CAMPAIGN 278

# CHERBOURG 1944

The first Allied victory in Normandy

**STEVEN J ZALOGA**

ILLUSTRATED BY STEVE NOON
*Series editor Marcus Cowper*

First published in Great Britain in 2015 by Osprey Publishing,
PO Box 883, Oxford, OX1 9PL, UK
PO Box 3985, New York, NY 10185-3985, USA
E-mail: info@ospreypublishing.com

ISBN: 978 1 4728 0663 5
E-book ISBN: 978 1 4728 0272 9
E-pub ISBN: 978 1 4728 0273 6

Editorial by Ilios Publishing Ltd, Oxford, UK (www.iliospublishing.com)
Index by Zoe Ross
Typeset in Myriad Pro and Sabon
Maps by Bounford.com
3D bird's-eye view by The Black Spot
Battlescene illustrations by Steve Noon
Originated by PDQ Media, Bungay, UK
Printed in China through Worldprint Ltd.

15 16 17 18 19   10 9 8 7 6 5 4 3 2 1

## AUTHOR'S NOTES

For brevity, the traditional conventions have been used when referring to
units. In the case of US units, 2/39th Infantry refers to the 2nd Battalion,
39th Infantry Regiment. The US Army traditionally uses Arabic numerals for
divisions and smaller independent formations (9th Division, 756th Tank
Battalion); Roman numerals for corps (VII Corps), spelled numbers for field
armies (First US Army) and Arabic numerals for army groups (12th Army
Group). In the case of German units, 2./GR 919 refers to the 2nd Company,
Grenadier-Regiment 919; II./GR 919 indicates the II Bataillon of Grenadier-
Regiment 919. German corps were designated with Roman numerals such
as LXXXIV Armee Korps, but the shortened version 84. AK is used here for
clarity. Field armies were designated in the fashion 7. Armee, but most
often abbreviated in the fashion AOK 7.

## ARTIST'S NOTE

Readers may care to note that the original paintings from which the colour
plates in this book were prepared are available for private sale. The
Publishers retain all reproduction copyright whatsoever. All enquiries
should be addressed to:

www.steve-noon.co.uk

The Publishers regret that they can enter into no correspondence upon this
matter.

## THE WOODLAND TRUST

Osprey Publishing are supporting the Woodland Trust, the UK's leading
woodland conservation charity, by funding the dedication of trees.

## GLOSSARY

| | |
|---|---|
| AOK | *Armeeoberkommando*: Army high command, common abbreviation for a German field army |
| AR | *Artillerie-Regiment* |
| *Festung* | Fortress |
| FJR | *Fallschirmjäger Regiment*: Paratrooper regiment |
| gem.Flak-Abt. | *gemischte Flak Abteilung*: Mixed anti-aircraft battalion |
| GR | *Grenadier-Regiment* |
| HKAR | *Heeres-Küsten-Artillerie-regiment*: Army coastal artillery regiment |
| KG | *Kampfgruppe*: Battle group, extemporized formation a few companies to a regiment or more in size |
| KVA | *Küsten Verteidigung Abschnitt*: Divisional coast defense sector |
| KVU | *Küsten Verteidigung Untergruppe*: Sub-divisional coast defense group |
| le.Flak-Abt. | *leichte Flak Abteilung*: Light anti-aircraft battalion |
| MAA | *Marine-Artillerie-Abteilung*: Navy artillery battalion |
| MG-Btl | *Maschinengewehr Bataillon*: Machine-gun battalion |
| MHI | Military History Institute, Army Historical Education Center, Carlisle Barracks, PA |
| MKB | *Marine-Küsten-Batterie*: Naval coast battery |
| NARA | National Archives and Records Administration, College Park, MD |
| OB West | *Oberbefehlshaber West*: High Command West (Rundstedt's HQ) |
| (o) | *ortsfest*: Suffix to Flak designations indicating fixed site unit |
| Pz-ers.u.ausb.Abt. | *Panzer-Ersatz-und-Ausbildung-Abteilung*: Tank replacement and training battalion |
| StP | *Stützpunkt*, Strongpoint (company-sized defense position) |
| Tobruk | A class of small bunkers with circular openings for a crew-served weapon |
| USCG | US Coast Guard |
| (v) | *verlegefähig*: Suffix to Flak unit designation indication semi-mobile |
| W | *Widerstandsnest:* Defense nest (platoon-sized defense position) |

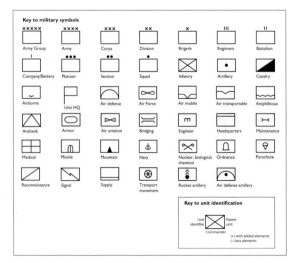

Key to military symbols

| | | | | | | |
|---|---|---|---|---|---|---|
| XXXXX | XXXX | XXX | XX | X | III | II |
| Army Group | Army | Corps | Division | Brigade | Regiment | Battalion |
| I | ••• | •• | • | | | |
| Company/Battery | Platoon | Section | Squad | Infantry | Artillery | Cavalry |
| Airborne | Unit HQ | Air defense | Air Force | Air mobile | Air transportable | Amphibious |
| Antitank | Armor | Air aviation | Bridging | Engineer | Headquarters | Maintenance |
| Medical | Missile | Mountain | Navy | Nuclear, biological, chemical | Ordnance | Parachute |
| Reconnaissance | Signal | Supply | Transport movement | Rocket artillery | Air defense artillery | |

Key to unit identification

Unit identifier — Parent unit
Commander
(+) with added elements
(−) less elements

# CONTENTS

# INTRODUCTION

The port city of Cherbourg was one of the most important objectives of the Allied armies following the D-Day landings on June 6, 1944. Although immediate logistical needs could be provided by over-the-beach delivery and the revolutionary Mulberry artificial harbors, the Allies needed a significant port for prolonged combat operations. Cherbourg was the most feasible port near the landing beaches, and its rapid capture was an essential Allied objective.

The Wehrmacht had presumed that any Allied landings in Lower Normandy (Basse Normandie) would require a port. As a result, both Cherbourg and Le Havre were heavily fortified in 1942–44 as part of the Atlantikwall program. This included the erection of an extensive network of coastal artillery batteries on both sides of the Cotentin Peninsula, extensive defenses in the immediate Cherbourg area, and a Landfront defense to the south of the city. On February 4, 1944, Hitler declared Cherbourg to be a *Festung* (fortress), which would be defended to the last man.

Following the landings at Utah Beach on D-Day, the German defenders of the Cotentin Peninsula frustrated American attempts to seize Cherbourg quickly by blocking an advance in the Montebourg sector. Since Cherbourg could not be captured on the run, on June 9, American commanders changed plans. They decided to cut off the Cotentin Peninsula to isolate the Cherbourg garrison from reinforcements from Brittany before proceeding to capture the port. After a shaky start in the difficult bocage country, VII Corps had pushed across the base of the Cotentin Peninsula by June 17. Rommel did not wish to have several divisions trapped on the Cotentin Peninsula, so three German divisions attempted to escape southward, leaving Kampfgruppe Schlieben to defend the city on its own. Over the course of the next week, VII Corps ground through the fortified Landfront defenses, reaching the outer ring of city defenses on June 21. The city fell on June 26, and the entire Cotentin Peninsula was declared secure on July 1, 1944.

An aerial reconnaissance photo of Cherbourg from the summer of 1944. (NARA)

# German dispositions on the Cotentin Peninsula: D-Day, June 6, 1944

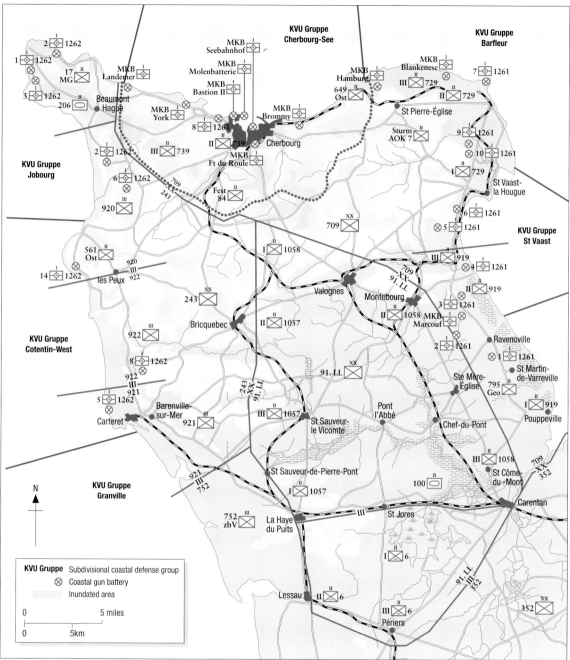

The German defenders had planned to conduct an extensive series of demolitions in the city to render the port useless. The demolition program was delayed by Hitler until the last minute, but succeeded in blocking most of the key port facilities. Anticipating such demolitions, the Allies moved special salvage units into the city to clear the port. Some limited use of the port began immediately, but it took about two months of reconstruction to return it to full potential.

# THE STRATEGIC SITUATION

Cherbourg had become an important port only in the 19th century after the construction of a series of artificial breakwaters and jetties to shelter the harbor from the harsh weather of the English Channel. By the turn of the century, it had become a vital international passenger hub for transatlantic liners. Its famous rail center connected passengers to Paris and the rest of continental Europe. Cherbourg was France's premier passenger port in the 1930s, but a distant 22nd for cargo with an average of only 900 tons per day.

Cherbourg had obvious military value, and the harbor was heavily fortified in the 19th century starting with Napoleon. Curiously enough, the Fashoda crisis of 1898 between Britain and France led to another spasm of construction – the modernization of the seaward bastions and the addition of a ring of forts on the landward side. Cherbourg saw brief military action in 1940. The British Expeditionary Force first used it as an embarkation port and, in June 1940, BEF units were evacuated from Cherbourg after Dunkirk fell. It was finally captured by Rommel's 7. Panzer-Division on June 19, 1940.

Early British planning for landings in France in 1942 such as Operation *Roundup* considered the seizure of a port as an essential ingredient. Cherbourg and Le Havre were the most likely Norman candidates, with Le Havre often favored because of the nearby airfields. Other schemes, such as the short-lived Operation *Sledgehammer*, considered the possibility of landing at Cherbourg and seizing the Cotentin Peninsula to provide an early foothold on the Continent. Cherbourg was the fifth-highest capacity port under Allied consideration after Antwerp, Rouen, Bordeaux, and Rotterdam, but the most attractive on account of its proximity to the Normandy beaches. It was anticipated that it could handle 5,000 tons of supplies daily within three months of capture; maximum capacity was expected to be about 8,500 tons daily after improvements were made.

A 37mm Flak 36 gun pit on the walls of Strongpoint 281 (Fort Central) in Cherbourg harbor with a coastal storm inundating the Digue Ouest breakwater in the background. This gun is still preserved at the fort today. (Alain Chazette)

# CHRONOLOGY

June 6       D-Day landings on Utah Beach.

June 7       German counterattack on Ste Mère-Église repulsed.

June 8       Rommel receives set of captured VII Corps orders, decides to reinforce Cotentin Peninsula.

June 10       90th Division begins attempt to cut off Cotentin Peninsula.

June 15       Failure of 90th Division leads to substitution of 9th Division and 82nd Airborne Division in westward attack.

June 16       Hitler meets Rommel and Rundstedt in France, insists on last-ditch defense of Cherbourg.

June 17       60th Infantry, 9th Division reaches the sea at Barneville, cutting off Cotentin Peninsula.

June 19       Final drive on Cherbourg begins as a three-division assault.

June 21       VII Corps reaches outer ring of defenses of Fortress Cherbourg.

June 25       US infantry begins entering outskirts of Cherbourg.

June 26       Senior Wehrmacht commanders in Cherbourg forced to surrender.

June 28       Final outlying German positions in Cherbourg harbor surrender.

June 30       Hold-outs on Cap de la Hague surrender to 9th Division.

July 1       9th Division reports that all organized German resistance on Cotentin Peninsula has ended.

# OPPOSING COMMANDERS

## GERMAN COMMANDERS

General der Artillerie Erich Marcks, commander of LXXXIV Armee Korps (84. AK). (Alain Chazette)

The supreme commander for German forces in the west (Oberbefehlshaber West) was **Generalfeldmarschall Gerd von Rundstedt**. His headquarters controlled two army groups in France, Heeresgruppe B on the invasion front in northern France, and Heeresgruppe G in central and southern France. Generalfeldmarschall Erwin Rommel was assigned to command Heeresgruppe B on the invasion front in the autumn of 1943. Rommel considerably invigorated the defense effort, and put his own stamp on the anti-invasion tactics.

Defense of the Cotentin Peninsula was the responsibility of the 7. Armee (AOK 7), commanded by **Generaloberst Friedrich Dollmann**. This field army controlled the French coast from the mouth of the Loire near St Nazaire eastward to the Pas-de-Calais and included all German Army units in Normandy and Brittany. Dollmann was a corps commander in Poland in 1939, and assigned command of AOK 7 in the Battle of France in 1940. He remained in command during the years of occupation. Some Eastern Front veterans serving in France felt that the years of occupation duty had softened him and his staff. Dollmann died of a heart attack on June 28, 1944, less than a month after D-Day.

The Lower Normandy sector, including the Cotentin Peninsula, was the responsibility of the LXXXIV Armee Korps (84. AK), commanded by General der Artillerie Erich Marcks. He served as a staff officer in Poland in 1939 and France in 1940. Marcks took part in the planning for Operation *Barbarossa*, and led the 101. Jäger-Division during the Russian campaign in 1941. He lost a leg in combat in March 1942, and, following his recuperation, was reassigned to lead the 337. Infanterie-Division. His skills as a divisional commander led to his elevation to corps command, first the 66. AK in September 1942, then the 87. AK. He was passed over by Hitler for field army command because of his connections to Gen. von Schleicher, murdered by the SS in 1934. Instead, he was reassigned to the 84. AK in France on August 1, 1943, as part of the process of refreshing the command structure in France with experienced Russian Front veterans. The 84. AK headquarters were located at St Lô. Marcks was killed in Normandy by an air attack on June 12, 1944.

The unit most closely associated with the defense of the Cotentin Peninsula was the 709. Infanterie-Division, commanded by **Generalleutnant Karl Wilhelm von Schlieben**. An infantry veteran of World War I, Schlieben had been most closely associated with the Panzer force, leading a *Panzergrenadier Regiment* of the 1. Panzer-Division in the Battle of France in 1940, a rifle brigade of the 4. Panzer-Division in 1942, and then 18. Panzer-Division during the battle of Kursk in 1943. The 18. Panzer-Division took such heavy casualties at Kursk that it was disbanded, and Schlieben was placed in reserve. He was appointed to command the 709. Infanterie-Division in December 1943 and was elevated to *Generalleutnant* on May 1, 1944. The division's headquarters were located in a bunker complex near the Château de Chiffrevast, to the north of Valognes.

The western side of the Cotentin Peninsula was defended by another static division, the 243. Infanterie- Division, commanded by **Generalleutnant Heinz Hellmich**. He led the 23. Infanterie-Division in France in 1940 and in Russia in 1941–42. After commanding a reserve division, he was assigned to lead the 243. Infanterie-Division on January 10, 1944. Hellmich was killed in an air attack on June 17, 1944.

The third Cotentin division, the newly formed 91. Luftlande-Division, had been commanded by **Generalleutnant Wilhelm Falley** since April 25, 1944. He had started the war as an infantry battalion commander, and led an infantry regiment in Russia in 1941 where he was awarded the Knight's Cross. After further service on the Russian front, he took over a succession of battered infantry divisions starting in September 1943. He was the first German general killed in Normandy after an encounter with US paratroopers in the pre-dawn hours of D-Day. Command was temporarily taken over by Generalmajor Bernhard Klosterkemper awaiting the arrival of a new commander, Generalmajor Eugen König, who was assigned the post on June 7.

The Cherbourg commandant was **Generalmajor Robert Sattler**. He was a decorated World War I veteran and served in the Reichswehr after the war. He commanded an infantry regiment in the early blitzkrieg campaigns of 1939–42. In 1942–44, he served in administrative and training roles until he was appointed to command Festung Cherbourg in April 1944. The senior Kriegsmarine

**LEFT**
Generalleutnant Heinz Hellmich, commander of the 243. Infanterie-Division and the later Kampfgruppe Hellmich. (MHI)
**RIGHT**
Generalleutnant Karl Wilhelm von Schlieben, commander of 709. Infanterie-Division (Bodenständig), and commander of Festung Cherbourg after June 23, 1944. (MHI)

**BELOW**
Generalmajor Robert Sattler was the commander of Festung Cherbourg until June 23 when Schlieben was appointed commander; Sattler then became his deputy. (NARA)

commander in Cherbourg was Konteradmiral Walter Hennecke who had served as Seekommandant Normandie since May 6, 1943. Hennecke began the war as commander of the light cruiser *Nürnberg* and in 1941 he was assigned to the old battleship *Schleswig-Holstein* . He was elevated to the rank of *Konteradmiral* (vice-admiral) on March 1, 1944. The Seekommandant Normandie had been formed in November 1941 and controlled naval forces on the French coast from Mont St Michel in the west to the Orne River estuary in the east. Besides commanding the various naval units based in Cherbourg and in smaller neighboring ports, the headquarters were also responsible for the extensive network of naval coastal artillery batteries in their sector. Hennecke was headquartered in the Villa Maurice in the Octeville suburb of Cherbourg.

## AMERICAN COMMANDERS

The First US Army was responsible for the conduct of the D-Day landings and was commanded by Lt. Gen. Omar Bradley. The VII Corps that landed at Utah Beach was commanded by **Maj. Gen. J. Lawton Collins.** He was known by his nickname, "Lightning Joe", derived from his divisional radio call sign on Guadalcanal. Collins graduated from West Point in April 1917, but did not arrive in Europe until after the Armistice. He received his first divisional command in May 1942, taking over the poorly trained 25th Division in the Pacific. Collins whipped it into shape for its first assignment, and it relieved the 1st Marine Division in Guadalcanal in early 1943. In 1944, the US Army chief of staff, Gen. George C. Marshall, began transferring seasoned officers back from the Pacific theater to provide units in Europe with more combat experience. Bradley later described Collins as "independent, heady, capable, and full of vinegar" and he would prove to be one of the most aggressive and talented US field commanders in Europe. Following his successes at Cherbourg, Collins led the US Army breakout from Normandy during Operation *Cobra* in July–August 1944, and was instrumental in crushing the 5. Panzerarmee in the Bastogne area during the Battle of the Bulge. He served as the US Army chief of staff during the Korean War.

With one exception, Collins was blessed with excellent divisional commanders. Not surprisingly, the two airborne division commanders were exceptional, but neither division figured prominently in the final Cherbourg campaign. The infantry division leading the assault on Utah Beach was the 4th Infantry Division, commanded by **Maj. Gen. Raymond "Tubby" Barton** since July 1942. Barton was a notoriously strict disciplinarian but he also proved to be an excellent trainer. He led the division through the autumn campaign, culminating in the ferocious Hürtgen Forest campaign that gutted the division. He was relieved

Major-General J. Lawton "Lightning Joe" Collins, commander of VII Corps. (NARA)

Major-General Raymond "Tubby" Barton, commander of the 4th Division is seen here at the wheel of his jeep "Barton Buggy." He is talking with Col. Charles T. Lanham, who took over command of the 22nd Infantry in July 1944 after Lt. Col. S. Brumby was wounded in action. (NARA)

for medical reasons by George Patton in December 1944. The 9th Infantry Division, headed by **Maj. Gen. Manton Eddy,** was a veteran of the North Africa and Sicily fighting and widely regarded as one of the Army's best divisions. Eddy was a particularly capable officer and in August 1944 was given command of XII Corps in Patton's Third Army. The 79th Division was commanded by **Maj. Gen. Ira Wyche,** West Point class of 1911. Wyche had served in the field artillery until assigned to command the 79th Division in May 1942, leading it in its combat debut in 1944.

Major-General Manton Eddy, commander of the 9th Infantry Division, seen here during the fighting in Cherbourg in June 1944. (NARA)

Of all the divisions in Collins' VII Corps, the only division to suffer from serious leadership problems was the 90th Division, led by **Maj. Gen. Jay MacKelvie.** An artilleryman, MacKelvie showed little affinity for infantry operations and was relieved by Collins on June 12 after five days of combat, along with two of his regimental commanders. His immediate replacement was a Pacific veteran, **Maj. Gen. Eugene Landrum,** who had commanded the 7th Infantry Division during the fighting with the Japanese in the Aleutian campaign. He was relieved by Bradley in August 1944 and was replaced by **Maj. Gen. Raymond S. McLain** in yet another shake-up in leadership of this troubled division.

# OPPOSING FORCES

## GERMAN FORCES

The Cotentin Peninsula received a variety of coastal defenses as part of the Atlantikwall program. Since Berlin felt that ports were the most likely Allied objectives, major harbors such as Cherbourg received the most extensive array of defenses. Cherbourg already had an extensive series of French naval fortifications, and these were substantially amplified by the German construction programs. Festung Cherbourg had its own command structure, led by Gen. Sattler. The city garrison had a single security battalion, II./Sicherungs-Rgt. 195, and a harbor company. Aside from regular army troops, 3,000 paramilitary construction troops of Organization Todt as well as portions of its 4,100-man naval garrison were assigned to armed *Alarmheiten* (emergency militia).

The shortage of motor transport on the Cotentin Peninsula led to the conversion of several infantry units including battalions of the Sturm-Abt. AOK 7 and 243. Infanterie-Division to bicycle transport. This is a heavy weapons company armed with the 88mm Panzerschreck anti-tank rocket launcher. (MHI)

The Cotentin coastline was defended by fortified coastal artillery positions. This was a more economical solution than large numbers of infantry units since a single gun battery could cover about 10km on either side. The coastal gun batteries were subordinate to Seekommandant Normandie when engaging naval targets, and control reverted to the Army once the batteries were targeted on Allied landing sites. The east coast of the Cotentin was shielded by the ten artillery batteries of HKAR 1261 (*Heeres-Küsten-Artillerie-Regiment*: Army coastal artillery regiment). The Kriegsmarine had a substantial coastal artillery force in and around Cherbourg harbor consisting of the nine batteries of MAA 260 (*Marine-Artillerie-Abteilung*: Navy artillery battalion). The western Cotentin coast starting at Cap de la Hague was covered by the Army's HKAR 1262 while the Navy's MAA 608 protected the port of Granville.

The coast defenses were divided into sectors starting with the divisional KVA coastal defense sectors (*Küsten Verteidigung Abschnitt*), which consisted of several KVU coastal defense subgroups (*Küsten Verteidigung Untergruppen*). The Cherbourg area was designated KVA-J and consisted of five subsectors, KVU-Jobourg to the west, KVU-Cherbourg-See for the harbor, KVU-Cherbourg-Land for the Landfront, and KVU Barfleur and KVU St Vaast on the eastern coast. When a second division was added to the Cotentin coast in May 1944, the defense sectors were bifurcated as KVA-J1 (709. Infanterie-Division) and KVA-J2 (243. Infanterie-Division).

Tactical infantry defenses along the coast were quite modest until Rommel's arrival in late 1943. Rommel insisted that more attention be paid to creating a network of infantry defense positions to stop the forthcoming Allied invasion on the beaches. The basic platoon-size *Widerstandsnesten* (defense nests) were combined to form a company-size *Stützpunkt* (strongpoint). Each defense nest usually had a field gun or anti-tank gun in a bunker, and several supporting mortars and machine guns in "Tobruk" concrete gun pits. There were usually a few underground bunkers for personnel and command posts, but most infantry positions were ordinary earthen trenches.

In spite of the many concrete bunkers and coastal defense guns, the actual fighting power of the Wehrmacht on the Cotentin Peninsula was hampered by lingering shortages of good quality troops. General Marcks summed up his opinion during the Cherbourg maneuvers in 1944: "Emplacements without guns, ammunition depots without ammunition, minefields without mines, and a large number of men in uniform with hardly a soldier among them." Major von der Heydte of Fallschirmjäger-Regiment 6 recalled, "The troops for a defense against an Allied landing were not comparable to those committed in Russia. Their morale was low; the majority of the enlisted men and noncommissioned officers lacked combat experience; and the officers were in the main those who, because of lack of qualification or on account of wounds or illness were no longer fit for service on the Eastern Front." The weapons were "from all over the world and seem to have been accumulated from all periods of the 20th century." Even if the German units on the Cotentin Peninsula were not the best in the Wehrmacht, they were still a credible fighting force. Training and tactics were based on hard-won battle experience, and there were Russian Front veterans in all of the divisions.

The division at the center of the defense of Cherbourg was the 709. Infanterie-Division. This division had been formed in May 1941 and was configured as a static (*Bodenständige*) division for occupation duties and coastal defense. It was originally deployed in Brittany and moved to the Cotentin Peninsula in December 1942. The static divisions lacked most organic transport, even horses. Rifle companies had only one horse for the commander and two draught horses for the field kitchens. Aside from its lack of mobility, the division also suffered from poor personnel allotment. The division was periodically combed for its most able troops who were transferred to the Russian front for combat duty. In October 1943, the entire 1. Bataillon/GR 739 was transferred to the Russian Front. This process left the division with over-age troops, soldiers with medical problems, and wounded veterans; in 1944 the average age of its troops was 36 years old. Until the autumn of 1943, it was usually understrength, with only 6,630 troops in June 1943. Like other static divisions in Normandy, it had an abnormally large number of Volksdeutsche troops. Early in the war, the Volksdeutsche

The principal tank support for the German units on the Cotentin Peninsula were two training and replacement battalions, Pz.-ers.u.ausb.Abt. 100 and Pz.-ers.u.ausb.Abt. 206, that were equipped with war-booty French tanks of 1940 vintage. Some of these are seen here in a US Army collection point near Isigny after the fighting. In the foreground is a turretless Renault R35, followed by several Hotchkiss H39s and a single Marder III from an infantry division anti-tank company. (NARA)

category referred to draftees of German ancestry from eastern Europe and the Balkans, including Romania and Hungary. Because of the desperate manpower shortages in 1943, a broader range of men were inducted, including Poles from the western provinces absorbed into the Reich, as well as Alsatians and other nationalities from the border regions, who had previously been excluded as unreliable. Although precise figures are lacking, the neighboring 716. Infanterie-Division had about 40 percent Volksdeutsche troops and the 709. Infanterie-Division was probably not much better.

Through the spring of 1944, the 709. Infanterie-Division was assigned to defend the entire coast of the Cotentin Peninsula from the Vire River estuary in the east to Montmartain on the western coast, a distance of some 250km (155 miles) plus an additional Landfront around Cherbourg adding a further inland perimeter of 65km (40 miles). Needless to say, this perimeter was grotesquely in excess of German tactical doctrine for a divisional sector. In practice, the division's combat elements were concentrated primarily around Cherbourg and the eastern coast on the presumption that the western coast was an unattractive landing site because of the currents and the German forces on the Channel Islands. The usual deployment was GR 739 in the Cherbourg area and GR 729 on the east Cotentin coast, the future Utah Beach.

Starting in the autumn of 1943, the division underwent a continual string of reorganizations to help prepare it to repel any Allied landings in the area. The most important addition was the transfer of GR 919 from the 242. Infanterie-Division, raising it to the normal three infantry regiments. It was the I. Bataillon from this regiment that manned the defenses around Utah Beach on D-Day. In early 1944, Georgische-Bataillon 729 was deployed to take over from the missing 1./GR 739. This battalion was made up of former Red Army prisoners of war from the Soviet republic of Georgia. Grenadier-Regiment 729 received Ost-Bataillon 649, made up primarily of Ukrainian troops. Two more eastern battalions, Georg.-Btl. 795, and Ost.-Btl. 549, were added in the spring. These eastern battalions were regarded as untrustworthy and the divisional commander remarked that it was too much to expect that former Soviet soldiers would "fight in France for Germany against the Americans." A later AOK 7 assessment concluded that their combat record was "good with one exception," presumably the performance of Georgische-Bataillon 729 near Utah Beach. A late addition on May 12, 1944, was MG-Bataillon 17, about 635 men - strong with a motorized pioneer platoon, a motorized *Panzerjäger* (tank destroyer) platoon with three 37mm guns, a mortar platoon and three heavy machine-gun companies. This unit was deployed initially to defend the Jobourg Peninsula.

In spite of the mediocre quality of the troops, by May 1944 the 709. Infanterie-Division was relatively large for a static division, with 12,655 men including about 2,155 Georgian and Ukrainian troops, and 335 unarmed Soviet "Hiwi" used for construction and non-combat roles. It had 11 infantry battalions instead of the nine found in the new pattern 1944 infantry divisions.

The extreme overextension of the 709. Infanterie-Division led Rommel to deploy more infantry to defend the Cotentin Peninsula. The next unit to arrive was the 243. Infanterie-Division. It had been organized in July 1943 as a static division and reorganized in January 1944 to a more conventional infantry formation. Two of its infantry battalions were converted from static units to bicycle infantry, though in the process, the division lost an infantry battalion. It was originally deployed in Lower Normandy in the Périers–Carentan area as corps reserve. After Rommel's inspection of the 709. Infanterie-Division on May 11, the division was forward deployed to defend the western coast taking over about 100km of coastline. On D-Day, it had a strength of about 11,530 troops, slightly understrength. The average age was 32 years old, and it contained about 30 percent Volksdeutsche, mainly Poles. Its artillery mostly consisted of captured Soviet types, but it had a self-propelled tank destroyer battalion with 14 75mm Marder III and ten StuG III assault guns. In early May 1944, the division was reinforced by Pz-ers.u.ausb.Abt. 206 (*Panzer-Ersatz-und-Ausbildung-Abteilung*), a tank training unit with obsolete war-booty French tanks.

On May 5, 1944, Gen. Dollmann proposed shifting the entire 74. AK from Brittany to the Cotentin, but this was rejected by Rommel. Hitler began to worry about the possibility of Allied landings in Normandy, and ordered that more paratrooper units be sent to the Cotentin. Instead, the 91. Luftlande-Division was transferred and arrived May 14, 1944. The 91. Luftlande-Division had been formed in January 1944 to take part in Operation *Tanne* (fir tree), an aborted airborne operation in Scandinavia planned for March 1944. Unlike the *Fallschirmjäger* paratrooper formations, it was a *Heer* (Army) formation rather than *Luftwaffe*.

Its configuration was somewhat similar to a *Gebirgsjäger* (mountain) division in that the equipment was tailored towards light weight and portability. At the time of the invasion, the partially formed division was understrength with only two infantry regiments and a single fusilier battalion, and numbered about 7,500 men. However, Fallschirmjäger-Regiment 6 (FR 6) from the 2. Fallschirmjäger Division was attached to the division during the Normandy fighting. Major von der Heydte

Flak batteries were widely deployed around Valognes because of the presence of several German headquarters in the town. This is a rare 50mm Flak 41, a failed type, of which there were only 24 still in service in 1944. It served with a battery in Yvetot-Bocage on the southern outskirts of Valognes. (MHI)

of FJR 6 considered that the combat efficiency of the 91. Luftlande-Division was poor, especially compared with his elite Luftwaffe troops. The division artillery was based around the 105mm Gebirgshaubitze 40 mountain gun, which did not share the same type of ammunition as the normal 105mm field howitzer, causing serious problems when its first allotment of ammunition was exhausted. The Pz-ers.u.ausb.Abt. 100 headquartered at Château de Francquetot provided the division with armored support.

There were a number of smaller formations in the area as well. Sturm-Abteilung AOK 7 was a bicycle-mobile infantry battalion attached to the AOK 7 headquarters that numbered 1,105 troops. Along with the FJR 6 paratroopers, its combat performance in June 1944 was later rated as "superior." On D-Day, it was shifted from Cherbourg southward to the battles near Utah Beach. Another late addition was schw.Stellungs-Werfer-Regiment 101 equipped with three battalions of rocket artillery, each with 18 schwere Wurfgerät 41 28/32 multiple rocket launchers with four launch racks per launcher. There was a motorized artillery regiment, Art.Regt. 621 with two motorized heavy artillery battalions, Artillerie-Abt. 456 (mot.) and Artillerie-Abt. 457 (mot.) equipped with 16 war-booty Soviet 152mm howitzers and eight Soviet 122mm guns. These units played an important role in the subsequent Cotentin fighting since much of the artillery of the 709. Infanterie-Division was tied down in coastal defense.

The Kriegsmarine used the port of Cherbourg as one of its two main bases to cover the Seine Bay, the other major base being Le Havre. The navy's main force consisted of two torpedo boat flotillas, Schnellboot-Flottille 5 and 9 totaling 16 S-boats, as well as a *Hafenschutzflottille* of small craft and barges. The harbor was extensively used for conducting mining operations off the Cotentin Peninsula. Following D-Day, the S-boats conducted frequent mining and torpedo actions against the invasion fleet. On the night of June 6–7, 14 S-boats sortied from Cherbourg, sinking a Royal Navy LST (landing ship tank) but losing two of their own to mines on the return trip. On the night of June 7–8, 11 S-boats sortied for operations in the Marcouf–Barfleur area, sinking two LCTs (landing craft tanks). On the night of June 8–9, they sank two LSTs. They continued in their raiding, but were reduced to only six boats by June 11 and the surviving boats were transferred to Le Havre by June 12. The Kriegsmarine attempted to reinforce the Cherbourg force on the night of June 8–9 by dispatching a corvette and three destroyers from Brest. Because of warnings from the Ultra decryption service, the force was intercepted at sea by the Royal Navy; two destroyers were sunk, one destroyer damaged and the two survivors retreated back to Brest.

Luftwaffe presence on the Cotentin Peninsula was modest, with only two airfields at Théville and Lessay, neither of which had any fighters in June 1944.

The field artillery batteries of the 91. Luftlande-Division were equipped with the Böhler 105mm Gebirgshaubitze 40 mountain gun, which used different ammunition from the normal 105mm lFh 18/40 field howitzer. After expending their available ammunition, the guns were useless because of the lack of suitable ammunition in the local supply network. (NARA)

# GERMAN UNITS, COTENTIN PENINSULA, JUNE 1944

| 84 ARMEE KORPS | ST LÔ | GENERAL DER ARTILLERIE ERICH MARCKS |
|---|---|---|
| Festung Cherbourg | Cherbourg | Gen.Maj. Robert Sattler |
| **709. Infanterie-Division** | **Château de Chiffrevast** | **Gen.Lt. Karl von Schlieben** |
| Grenadier-Regiment 729 | Le Vicel | Oberst Helmuth Rohrbach |
| Grenadier-Regiment 739 | Querqueville | Oberst Walther Köhn |
| Grenadier-Regiment 919 | Montebourg | Obstlt. Günther Keil |
| **243. Infanterie-Division** | **Château de Malassis** | **Gen.Lt. Heinz Hellmich** |
| Grenadier-Regiment 920 | Etoupeville | Oberst Bernhard Klosterkemper |
| Grenadier-Regiment 921 | Mauger | Obstlt. Jacob Simon |
| Grenadier-Regiment 922 | Haquets | Obstlt. Franz Müller |
| **91. Luftlande-Division** | **Château Haut de Bernaville** | **Gen.Maj. Wilhelm Falley** |
| Grenadier-Regiment 1057 | Hauteville | Oberst Sylvester von Saldern |
| Grenadier-Regiment 1058 | Vindefontaine | Oberst Kurt Beigang |
| Fallschirmjäger-Regiment 6 | Le Hôtellerie | Major Friedrich-August von der Heydte |
| **Corps units** | | |
| Sturm-Bataillon AOK 7 | Le Vicel | Major Hugo Messerschmidt |
| Flak-Regiment 30 | Cherbourg | Oberst Ernst Hermann |
| Artillerie-Regiment z.b.V. 621 | Bricquebec | Obstlt. Hermann Seidel |
| schw.Stellungs-Werfer-Regiment 101 | Vasteville | Major Rasmer |
| Pz-ers.u.ausb.Abteilung 100 | Franquetot | Major Berdtenschlager |
| Pz-ers.u.ausb.Abteilung 206 | Auderville | Major Ernst Wenk |
| MG-Bataillon 17 | Beaumont-Hague | Major Hans Reichert |

## COASTAL ARTILLERY UNITS

| **HKAR 1261** | **Le Poteau** | **Oberst Gerhard Treipel** |
|---|---|---|
| 1./ HKAR 1261 | St Martin-de-Varreville | 4x 122mm K390/2 (r) |
| 2./ HKAR 1261 | Azeville | 4 x 105mm K331 (f) |
| 3./ HKAR 1261 | Fontenay | 6 x 155mm K418 (f) |
| 4./ HKAR 1261 | Quinéville | 4 x 105mm K331 (f) |
| 5./ HKAR 1261 | Crasville | 4 x 105mm K331 (f) |
| 6./ HKAR 1261 | Morsalines | 6 x 155mm K416 (f) |
| 7./ HKAR 1261 | Gatteville | 6 x 155mm K420 (f) |
| 8./ HKAR 1261 | Les Couplets | 6 x 155mm K420 (f) |
| 9./ HKAR 1261 | La Pernelle I | 6 x 105mm K331 (f) |
| 10./ HKAR 1261 | La Pernelle II | 3 x 170mm K18 |
| **HKAR 1262** | **Sotteville** | **Major Hubert Otte** |
| 1./ HKAR 1262 | Auderville-la-Roche | 6 x 155mm K416 (f) |
| 2./ HKAR 1262 | Biville | 4 x 105mm K331 (f) |
| 3./ HKAR 1262 | Auderville-Laye | 2 x 20.3cm K (E) |
| 4./ HKAR 1262 | Cap Flamanville | 4 x 170mm K18 |
| 5./ HKAR 1262 | Cap Carteret | 4 x 122mm K390/1 (r) |
| **Marineartillerieabteilung 260** | **Les Capelins** | **Kapitänleutnant Karl Weise** |
| MKB Marcouf | St Marcouf | 4 x 210mm K39/41, 1x 150mm SKL/45 |
| MKB Blankenese | Néville | 4 x 94mm Vickers M39 (e) |
| MKB Hamburg | Fermanville | 4 x 240mm SKL/40 |
| MKB Brommy | Les Caplains | 4 x 150mm SKC/28 |
| MKB Fort du Roule | Fort du Roule | 4 x 105mm SKC/32 u |
| MKB Bastion | L'Arsenal | 4 x 105mm SKC/32 u |
| MKB Yorck | Anfreville | 4 x 170mm SKL/40 |
| MKB Landemer | Castel-Vendon | 4x 150mm SKC/28 |
| MKB Gréville | Castel-Vendon | 2 x 38cm SKC/34 |

# AMERICAN FORCES

The 82nd and 101st Airborne Divisions landed behind Utah Beach in the early morning hours of June 6, 1944, at the extreme right flank of the Allied landings. Although the parachute and glider landings substantially disrupted German defenses behind Utah Beach, the night drops had not been precise and both divisions were badly scattered and had limited tactical coherence. The 82nd Airborne Division took part in the fighting to expand the Utah Beach beachhead around Ste Mére-Église and the Mederet River, while the 101st Airborne Division operated farther to the southeast in the Carentan sector as part of the VII Corps effort to link up with V Corps from Omaha Beach.

The 4th Infantry Division landed at dawn on Utah Beach against light German resistance and quickly pushed off the beach. This division had been reactivated in 1940 and at first was equipped as a motorized infantry division. This configuration was eventually abandoned, and the division reverted to a conventional organization in August 1943 prior to being sent to England. While Bradley had insisted on using at least one experienced division in the assault at neighboring Omaha Beach, Utah Beach was viewed as a less demanding mission. Nevertheless, it required the use of a well-trained and ably led division, and the 4th Division was chosen. Armored support for the division came from the 70th Tank Battalion, the most experienced separate tank battalion in the US Army, which had previously seen combat as a light tank battalion in North Africa and Sicily.

In the build-up immediately after D-Day, three more infantry divisions were gradually injected into the Cotentin fighting. The 90th Division was based around National Guard units raised in the Texas–Oklahoma area,

The VII Corps had several tank and tank destroyer battalions for infantry support in the Cotentin fighting. This is an M4 medium tank of Company B, 746th Tank Battalion on the road south of the naval hospital supporting the 47th Infantry in the fighting in Cherbourg on June 26. (NARA)

hence its nickname "Tough Ombres" from the time of its service in World War I. It developed a bad reputation in Normandy because of poor leadership and it was subjected to a series of leadership changes; by late summer the problems had been ironed out and it fought with distinction with Patton's Third Army in Lorraine in September 1944. The 9th Division was widely regarded as one of the army's best infantry divisions, with previous combat experience in North Africa and Sicily. The 79th Division was activated in 1942 and shipped to Britain in April 1944. It was a fairly typical US infantry division with good training and leadership.

One of the most significant Allied advantages was the availability of continual air support. At this stage of the war, cooperation between ground and air units was still in a formative stage, and did not come to fruition until late July during Operation *Cobra*. Nevertheless, continual air operations over the Cotentin Peninsula by roving fighter-bombers made any concentrated daytime movement by German units impossible. Another Allied advantage was the presence of the US Navy and Royal Navy in the waters off Normandy. These provided heavy fire support in the days after the D-Day landings.

## US ARMY, COTENTIN PENINSULA, JUNE 1944

| VII CORPS | MAJ. GEN. J. LAWTON COLLINS |
|---|---|
| **4th Division** | **Maj. Gen. Raymond Barton** |
| 8th Infantry | Col. James Van Fleet |
| 12th Infantry | Col. Russell Reeder |
| 22nd Infantry | Lt. Col. Sewell Brumby |
| **9th Division** | **Maj. Gen. Manton Eddy** |
| 39th Infantry | Col. Harry "Paddy" Flint |
| 47th Infantry | Col. George Smythe |
| 60th Infantry | Col. Frederick de Rohan |
| **79th Division** | **Maj. Gen. Ira Wyche** |
| 313th Infantry | Col. Sterling Wood |
| 314th Infantry | Col. Warren Robinson |
| 315th Infantry | Col. Poter Wiggins |
| **90th Division** | **Brig. Gen. Jay MacKelvie** |
| 357th Infantry | Col. Philip Ginder |
| 358th Infantry | Col. James Thompson |
| 359th Infantry | Col. Clarke Fales |
| **Corps Units** | |
| 4th Cavalry Group | Col. Joseph Tully |
| 4th Cavalry Squadron | Lt. Col. E. C. Dunn |
| 24th Cavalry Squadron | Lt. Col. F. H. Gaston Jr. |
| 6th Armored Group | Col. Francis Fainter |
| 70th Tank Battalion | Lt. Col. John Welbron |
| 746th Tank Battalion | Lt. Col. C. G. Hupfer |

# OPPOSING PLANS

## GERMAN PLANS

German planning through the end of 1943 presumed that the Allied amphibious landings would strike across the narrowest portion of the Channel against the Pas-de-Calais. A reassessment of this issue by Rundstedt's OB West headquarters in January 1944 leaned towards the Pas-de-Calais, but also highlighted potential landing sites in Lower Normandy. The two most likely landing areas were judged to be Cherbourg and Le Havre, based on the German view that harbors were the most likely objective. During his tour of the Altantikwall in February 1944, Rommel visited the Grandcamp sector, the future Omaha Beach, and recognized the similarities of this sector to the Allied landing beaches at Salerno in September 1943. One of the reasons for his concern was that the Vire River estuary offered a variety of small harbors and also served as the eastern end of the Cotentin Peninsula, and so was a likely point to initiate any operation to cut off Cherbourg. His concerns about this sector led to the deployment of the 352. Infanterie-Division on the eastern side of the Vire River estuary and the reinforcement of the forces in the Cotentin elbow.

Hitler began to have premonitions that the Allies might land somewhere other than the Pas-de-Calais. During a speech to German commanders in France on March 20, 1944, he suggested, "The most suitable and so most threatened areas are the two peninsulas in the west, Cherbourg and Brest, which are very tempting and offer the best possibilities for forming a beachhead." Vizeadmiral Theodor Krancke, commander of the Kriegsmarine Marine-Gruppekommando West, noticed from reconnaissance photos that there was no activity in the ports of southeastern England or the mouth of the Thames and so his assessment from April 26, 1944, discounted the risk to the Pas-de-Calais. Allied bombing and mine-clearing operations also suggested that the landings would come between Cherbourg and Boulogne, most likely the Cotentin Peninsula, the Seine estuary near Le Havre or the mouth of the Somme. He later noticed that Le Havre and Cherbourg had not been heavily bombed, which led him to believe that these two ports were the most likely objectives.

The changing appreciation of the threat in the spring of 1944 led to German reinforcement of the Cotentin Peninsula, increasing the forces there from one division to three by May 1944; there was an additional division on the Channel Islands off the western coast. The western Cotentin coast had been lightly guarded since the Kriegsmarine had argued that the heavy seas, as well as the heavily defended Channel Islands, made amphibious landings unlikely. In mid-May, the Navy staff had a change of heart, and began to suggest that the Allies might land on both the east and west coasts, with simultaneous attacks on either side of Cherbourg. Shortly afterwards, Rommel visited the area, and later had a conference with Dollmann and Marcks about the state of defenses in this sector. In May 1944, Schlieben argued that the port facilities in Cherbourg should be sabotaged immediately to make the port an unattractive target, and to permit units to withdraw to the base of the Cotentin Peninsula rather than becoming trapped. The Navy would not even consider such a plan and Schlieben's proposal was ignored.

Wargames by AOK 7 in 1943–44 had studied the options for landings on the Cotentin Peninsula. These concluded that the two most likely landing sites would be the eastern beaches near the Vire River (the future Utah Beach) or the Jobourg Peninsula (Cap de la Hague) to the west of Cherbourg. Landings in the immediate Cherbourg area were viewed as unlikely because of the extensive cliffs along the coast, as well as the heavy concentration of coastal guns. The Army remained skeptical about the vulnerability of the west coast. Since the 709. Infanterie-Division was already heavily concentrated along the eastern coast, the AOK 7 reinforced the northwestern corner of the Cotentin Peninsula as more forces became available in the spring of 1944. When the 91. Luftlande-Division became available in May because of Hitler's concerns, it was placed in the center of the peninsula as a corps reserve that could be committed either towards the eastern coast or the Jobourg Peninsula depending on actual Allied actions.

One of the central dilemmas in German planning both before and after the D-Day invasion was the operational mobility of Allied forces provided both by naval and air superiority. Allied naval dominance meant that the Allies could land nearly anywhere on the French coast. Not only did this affect deployments prior to the D-Day landings, but German commanders were constrained in moving units from the Pas-de-Calais or other locations to reinforce the Cherbourg Peninsula later in June for fear that the Allies would conduct subsequent landings after D-Day.

German anti-invasion plans focused on the ports. As a result, Cherbourg and Le Havre were the most intensely defended points in lower Normandy. Cherbourg harbor was protected by numerous gun batteries including this R650 bunker armed with a war-booty French 75mm Flak M22-24(f) with an additional 20mm Flak cannon on the roof. This gun casemate was part of MKB Seebahnhof, located on the pier in front of the Gare Maritime. (NARA)

# AMERICAN PLANS

The defeat of the Dieppe raid in August 1942 and the German fortification of the Normandy ports during the Atlantikwall construction convinced Allied planners to conduct the amphibious landings against the weakly defended Normandy beaches away from the ports. By early 1943, planners had selected the Caen area as the focus of the attack. While Le Havre remained attractive, the need to ford the Seine River to secure Le Havre reduced its appeal as a short-term objective. Cherbourg became the default solution for quick capture. It was recognized from the outset that it lacked the capacity to support the 29 Allied divisions expected in the lodgment area by the late summer of 1944. As a result, the *Overlord* plan was enlarged to encompass the eventual capture of additional ports after Cherbourg, most notably ports in Brittany such as Brest and Quiberon Bay, or the Seine River ports such as Le Havre and Rouen.

The capture of Cherbourg was the primary mission of the US Army forces landing in Normandy. The original objective was to secure Cherbourg by D+14, by which time 18 Allied divisions would be ashore. The planned capture of Cherbourg was later pushed back to D+15 as Allied intelligence discovered the addition of new German units on the Cotentin Peninsula. The deployment of the 91. Luftlande-Division in the central Cotentin Peninsula was discovered in mid-May 1944.

The VII Corps Field Orders released on May 28, 1944, outlined the tactical approach to secure Cherbourg. The VII Corps planned to push northward out of the beachhead with a single division along the Montebourg–Valognes axis using the Douve River as a shield on its left flank. Early plans assumed a quick advance on Cherbourg since German forces on the Cotentin Peninsula were so weak during the first months of 1944. At the time of the D-Day landings, there was no plan to cut off the Cotentin Peninsula as would eventually occur.

Eisenhower's concern over the junction of VII Corps from Utah Beach and V Corps from Omaha Beach led to a change of plans, with the focus shifting away from a rapid assault on Cherbourg to a junction of the two corps around Carentan in the first week after D-Day. Collins (left) discusses plans with Eisenhower and Bradley. (NARA)

# THE CAMPAIGN

## EXPANDING THE BEACHHEAD

Grenadier-Regiment 919 of the 709. Infanterie-Division defended the coast that included Utah Beach with 3./GR 919 deployed on Utah Beach itself. This company was quickly overcome on D-Day. Following the D-Day landings, the 4th Infantry Division pushed off Utah Beach in a northwesterly direction, intending to advance towards Cherbourg. Both the 82nd and 101st Airborne Divisions were badly dispersed behind Utah Beach and it would take days to consolidate the scattered paratroopers.

On June 7, D+1, the focus of the 4th Infantry Division was to deal with German forces around Ste Mère-Église and to try to push up the coastal road to the north. The situation in Ste Mère-Église was chaotic since paratroopers of the 82nd Airborne Division were active in the city, while at the same time a variety of German units had been attempting to recapture the town since D-Day. Georgian troops of the Georg.-Btl. 795 had been deployed to the east and south of Ste Mère-Église and had been joined by various elements of I./GR 919 that had retreated from the beach area. Sturm-Abteilung AOK 7 had been ordered to attack the town on D-Day, and GR 1058 from the 91. Luftlande-Division was also moving to the scene. A battle group under Lt. Ogroske including several Marder I tank destroyers of Panzerjäger-Abt. 709 were sent to reinforce this attack. They passed through Azeville without infantry support and were beaten up by paratrooper 57mm anti-tank guns on the outskirts of Ste Mère-Église on D-Day. Grenadier-Regiment 1058, supported by StuG III assault guns of Panzerjäger-Abt. 243, made further attempts to break into Ste Mère-Église on June 7, but were beaten back by the actions of the paratroopers, the 8th Infantry (4th Division) and a company of M4 tanks from the 746th Tank Battalion. The 8th Infantry established defensive positions to the north and west of the town by late on June 7.

The lead element of the 243. Infanterie-Division to reach the Utah Beach area was Oberleutnant Franz Fallnich's Panzerjäger-Abt. 243. They lost several of their StuG III assault guns in skirmishes with the 82nd Airborne Division around Ste Mère-Église in the days after D-Day. (MHI)

The 82nd Airborne was reinforced that morning by additional air-landings of the 325th Glider Infantry in the area of Le Forge. Besides the fighting around Ste Mère-Église, the 82nd Airborne Division was heavily involved in efforts to secure the bridges over the Mederet River in order to push the beachhead farther west. Grenadier-Regiment 1057 of the 91. Luftlande-Division attempted to contain the paratroopers by attacking from the west. The fighting on June 7 solidified the positions of the 82nd Airborne Division and firmly connected it to the seaborne invasion force.

While the 8th Infantry was heavily engaged around Ste Mère-Église, the 4th Division's other two regiments pushed northward out of the beachhead along the coast. The most difficult fighting took place around the fortified German coastal gun positions at Azeville (2./HKAR 1261) and Crisbecq (MKB Marcouf). Aside from the fortified gun casemates, these batteries had a significant number of other defensive fortifications and they had also accumulated infantry troops who had retreated from the beaches. Although the 12th and 22nd Infantry Regiments were able to push about 2 miles northward during the day, they were unable to overcome the two fortified areas and suffered heavy casualties in the process.

The 3rd Battalion, 22nd Infantry advanced northward along the coast and reduced the surviving German beach defense nests. Naval fire control parties helped direct the gunfire of warships against the bunkers. By the evening of D+1, the battalion had fought its way through all of the German defenses up to W11 when it was ordered inland to serve as a reserve for the other two battalions of the 22nd Infantry that had been battered that day in the fighting with the coastal artillery fortifications.

The 101st Airborne Division was involved in securing the southern flank of the beachhead, especially around Saint-Côme-du-Mont and the Douve River north of Carentan. It was mainly engaged against Fallschirmjäger-Regiment 6. Since the focus of this book is on Cherbourg, this sector will not be treated in detail in this book.[1]

By the end of June 7, the German defenses around the American beachhead were hard pressed. Grenadier-Regiment 1058, facing the 4th Division around Ste Mère-Église, had been badly beaten up and its commander killed. The neighboring GR 1057 along the Mederet was being steadily pushed back by the 82nd Airborne Division. The I./GR 919 of the 709. Infanterie-Division had been badly disrupted by the Utah Beach landings. Schlieben was reluctant to redeploy the regiment's other two battalions positioned in the beach defenses north of Utah Beach because of a conviction that the Americans would conduct additional amphibious landings farther up the coast over the next few days.

Recognizing the weakness of the local forces, the 84. AK commander, Gen. Marcks, had already instructed the 243. Infanterie-Division on the western coast to mobilize one of its regiments and to send it to the Ste Mère-Église sector. Marcks fully expected that the objective of the Utah Beach landings was to capture Cherbourg, and so he considered the Montebourg–Valognes axis to be the main focal point (*Schwerpunkt*) of the operation. Marcks consulted with Schlieben and authorized him to move GR 729 from its defensive position on the northeastern coast to join with the other units

---

1  The fighting towards Carentan is covered in Campaign 104, *D-Day 1944 (2): Utah Beach and the US Airborne Landings* (Osprey: 2004).

trying to block the Montebourg–Valognes axis. Owing to the lack of sufficient horses or vehicles in the 709. Infanterie-Division, the 30km movement of this regiment would be time-consuming. Furthermore, the roads were under constant patrol by Allied fighters, which severely constrained daylight marches. In addition, they would be faced with a logistics problem once redeployed since they had no transport for moving supplies. The blocking force along the Ste Mère-Église–Montebourg axis was also supported by available corps heavy artillery including Art.Regt. 621 and Stellungswerfer-Regt. 101.

Although VII Corps had made solid progress on June 7 (D+1), it was behind schedule. During a visit to Normandy on D+1, Eisenhower expressed his concern to Bradley that the Germans might exploit the gap between V Corps on Omaha Beach and VII Corps on Utah. Bradley instructed Collins to focus his immediate attention on closing this gap by seizing Carentan in the south and to deal with Cherbourg later. As a result, all of the resources of the 101st Airborne Division were used in this direction, along with elements of the 82nd Airborne Division. It would take nearly a week of hard fighting, until June 14, before a junction was made between V Corps and VII Corps.

# THE BATTLE FOR THE GUN BATTERIES

The northward attack on June 8 (D+2) on the western side of the Ste Mère-Église–Montebourg road involved the 8th Infantry of the 4th Division with four battalions from the 82nd Airborne Division (505th PIR and 2/325th GIR) on the extreme left flank. The terrain in this sector had typical Norman hedgerows, but they were spaced more widely apart than in other sectors. They provided an excellent basis for defensive lines, held mainly by remnants of GR 1058. The attack proved more difficult than expected, gaining only about 1,500 yards. German accounts attribute this mainly to the heavy artillery fire offered by AR 621 and the newly arrived batteries of III./AR 243. The 3/8th Infantry had a particularly hard time around the French airship hangar near Écausseville after the sector was reinforced by the bicycle troops of Sturm-Abt. AOK 7.

On the eastern side of the Ste Mère-Église–Montebourg road, the 22nd Infantry was still stymied by the extensive fortifications of the coastal artillery batteries in this sector. The 1/22nd Infantry assaulted the MKB Marcouf battery (MAA 260) while 2/22nd Infantry assaulted the Azeville battery (2./HKAR 1261). MKB Marcouf, known as the "Crisbecq battery" in American accounts, had been the most active on this section of the coast. It sank the destroyer USS *Corry* on D-Day and fired on Utah Beach. It had continued to exchange

This is the second casemate of the Azeville battery, 2./HKAR 1261, an R650 bunker armed with a war-booty French 105mm K.331(f) field gun. Extensive shellfire damage caused by naval fire and tank guns can be seen around the embrasure. (NARA)

fire with US battleships and cruisers for several days, losing one of its guns to a direct hit from the battleship USS *Nevada* on D-Day morning. Commanded by Oberleutnant (MA) Walther Ohmsen, the battery had about 315 Navy artillerymen reinforced by the infantry of 6./GR 919, as well as the troops from defense nests W14 and W14a who were withdrawn from the beach on June 8, and many stragglers from strongpoints farther south along the coast. In total, it had more than 400 troops. Aside from its main armament of four Škoda 210mm naval guns, the battery also had a 150mm naval gun, six French 75mm anti-aircraft guns and four 20mm Flak guns. The main guns had been in open kettle pits until early in 1944 when a program was begun to encase them in large R683 bunkers. This process was not complete because of bombing attacks, which cratered the site. The site had perimeter defense provided by a number of machine guns mounted in small concrete Tobruk bunkers.

The neighboring battery at Azeville was an army unit commanded by Lt. Hans Kattnig and armed with four French 105mm guns and two 37mm Flak guns with about 170 troops. Besides its gun crews, it had been reinforced by a rifle platoon from 3./GR 922. Both batteries were in communication with one another through buried landlines. The Azeville battery was able to fire on the Marcouf battery since most of the German defenders were protected in concrete bunkers and preparations had been made before the invasion by using such tactics as a means to clear the battery site of American infantry.

The attack by 1/22nd Infantry against the Marcouf battery on June 7 reached the southern perimeter of the battery. However, the southern sector of the battery included most of the site's anti-aircraft guns. The rapid-fire 75mm anti-aircraft guns and 20mm cannons were very effective against the attacking infantry. In addition, the first reinforcements from the 243. Infanterie-Division had begun arriving in this sector the previous day.

A contemporary view of the third casemate of the Azeville battery in the foreground and the fourth casemate in the background. The fourth casemate had an additional structure on the roof with a 37mm Flak gun. (Author's photograph)

On the morning of June 7, Kampfgruppe Müller, consisting of two infantry battalions and the divisional engineer battalion from the 243. Infanterie-Division, attacked and recaptured the town of St Marcouf. That evening, the battery was bombarded by Allied naval gunfire and US Army artillery. The attack on MKB Marcouf resumed on June 8. The 1/22nd Infantry captured the village of St Marcouf and penetrated the battery positions. The US infantry was armed with pole charges, and began attacking the concrete shelters that the German troops were using as fighting positions. By late afternoon, the American infantry had nearly reached the main gun casemates, so Ohmsen called on Kattnig to have the Azeville battery pummel the fortified battery positions. This succeeded in halting the 1/22nd Infantry, and Lt. Geissler from the 6./GR 919 led a counterattack which pushed the 1/22nd Infantry back about a mile from the battery, taking nearly a hundred prisoners in the process. The 2/22nd Infantry did not have any more success against the Azeville battery on June 7–8, and suffered casualties from rocket artillery fire from Stellungswerfer-Regt. 101. The regiment's remaining battalion, 3/22nd Infantry, continued to push northward along the beach to eliminate remaining strongpoints being held by GR 919.

Even though the assorted German units holding the Montebourg sector had held back the Americans another day, personnel losses had been high. Among the casualties that day were the commander of GR 1058, Oberst Kurt Beiging, and the commander of III./GR 739, Maj. Ebrecht. The Sturm-Abt. AOK 7 went from an initial strength of about 1,100 men to an effective strength of only 100 after two days of intense fighting.

On June 8, German troops near Utah Beach found a copy of VII Corps' operations orders from a sunken landing craft. This was delivered to Schlieben, and copies were quickly sent to Marcks and Rommel. As Schlieben and Marcks had expected, the American plan was to push out of the beachhead along the Montebourg axis with the primary objective being the capture of Cherbourg. In a phone conversation between Marcks and Schlieben, the corps commander again re-emphasized that the Montebourg axis was the key to the defense of Cherbourg. Rommel had originally believed that the main Allied effort would be on the Calvados coast, especially in the British sector around Caen. After reading the captured American orders, he began to realize the centrality of Cherbourg to the Allied plans. As a result, he ordered one of his few reserves, the 77. Infanterie-Division, to change its intended destination. He had originally planned to move it from its base near St Malo into the Carentan battle to prevent the juncture of V Corps and VII Corps. Instead, he ordered it to Valognes to reinforce the Montebourg defenses.

In view of the strong defense of MKB Marcouf, the 4th Infantry Division changed its approach on June 9. Instead of dispersing the battalions of the 22nd Infantry against different objectives, they concentrated most of the regiment plus supporting elements into Task Force A. The objective was to brush past the two German fortified areas to reach the main objective of the Quinéville ridge. The task force, led by the assistant division commander, Brig. Gen. Henry Barber, was reinforced with two medium tank companies from the 70th Tank Battalion, a light tank platoon from the 746th Tank Battalion, two companies of M10 tank destroyers of the 899th Tank Destroyer Battalion, and the 4th Engineer Combat Battalion. MKB Marcouf would be contained by Co. C, 22nd Infantry, supported by the remaining company of M10 tank destroyers.

The German defenses were pummeled by naval gunfire the night before the attack. The battleship USS *Nevada* engaged MKB Marcouf with its 14in. guns, scoring one hit through the embrasure of No. 4 casemate that killed the crew. This was followed on the morning of June 9 with a barrage of 1,500 rounds by the 44th Field Artillery Battalion.

The 3/22nd Infantry led the attack. Company L was assigned to clear out the village of Azeville while Company I headed towards the rear side of the Azeville battery. The accompanying tanks of the 70th Tank Battalion, except for one, were halted by minefields. The single M4 tank began to engage the bunkers. Direct hits against the gun embrasures knocked out most of the surviving guns, and the battery commander, Lt. Kattnig, was wounded when an M4 medium tank began firing at the Flak gun position where he was stationed. An assault team attempted to open up the southernmost gun casemate, Turm 1, using high explosives against the armored door at the rear. This failed, but a flame-thrower attack through the armored door ignited small arms ammunition stored in the bunker, threatening to ignite the main artillery charges. Sending out a captured US paratrooper officer under a white flag, the battery surrendered. Of the original 253 German troops, 78 were killed and 161 surrendered, while the others escaped or were missing.

At 1630hrs, Task Force A set out for its initial objective of Ozeville in front of the Quinéville ridge, led by the tanks of Co. B, 70th Tank Battalion. The advance progressed as far as the Château de Fontenay where it was stopped by the III./GR 922 with heavy artillery support. By this stage, the 709. Infanterie-Division had concentrated its anti-tank guns, including those from the regimental batteries, under Hauptmann Rümrich's Panzerjager-Abt. 709. This unit was moved around as occasion demanded to deal with American tank attacks, and it was in the Château de Fontenay sector during this attack. The Germans claimed to have knocked out 17 tanks, partly from the anti-tank guns but also from infantry anti-tank rockets; actual US losses were two medium tanks.

This is one of the two completed R683 bunkers of MKB Marcouf; the other two gun casemates were not yet complete at the time of the June 1944 fighting. This battery was armed with four Škoda 210mm K.39/41 guns and the site is seen after its capture with extensive damage to the face of the bunker. (NARA)

The delays imposed by the Azeville and Marcouf batteries provided Schlieben with the time to reinforce the Montebourg front. On June 9, while the fighting was going on around Azeville, he was granted permission from Dollmann's AOK 7 headquarters to shift two more battalions from the 243. Infanterie-Division to the Montebourg defenses, II./GR 921 and I./GR 922. While Schlieben was denied the transfer of MG-Bataillon 17 from the Jobourg Penisula to Montebourg, he was allotted most of the light tanks of Pz.-Abt. 206. Schlieben also requested that the Luftwaffe attack the Allied warships off the coast that had taken part in the bombardment of German defenses around the city. Although there were Luftwaffe attacks against the Allied fleet, they had negligible effect in this sector. Rommel was reluctant to reinforce the Montebourg front too strongly on the presumption that the Allies would simply stage an amphibious landing farther north along the Cotentin coast behind Montebourg near Vauville, or conduct airborne landings behind the Montebourg line near Valognes or Cherbourg itself.

The 4th Infantry Division continued its push on Montebourg on June 10 using all three regiments with the 8th Infantry on the left, the 12th Infantry in the center and Task Force A on the right. Task Force A continued to have difficulties on account of the crust of fortified positions close to the coast. Ozeville had another entrenched artillery position that had been abandoned more than a year before, but it was occupied by Kampfgruppe Müller and held out against repeated attacks. The 8th Infantry's attacks to the west of Montebourg succeeded in dislodging the newly arrived II./GR 921, which retreated after its commander was killed.

MKB Marcouf continued to defend the perimeter on June 9–10 against a small American containing force and by this point had lost 307 men from the original garrison of about 400. By the morning of July 11, it was nearly out of ammunition so Ohmsen was given permission to withdraw. Under the cover of darkness, the surviving 78 men escaped, leaving behind 21 wounded and 126 American prisoners. Ohmsen had already been awarded two Iron Crosses for his previous actions at Marcouf, and after his escape he was decorated with the Knight's Cross.

While the 22nd Infantry was containing the Azeville and Marcouf batteries, the other two regiments of the 4th Infantry Division continued to push forward to Montebourg. The town itself was commanded by Hauptmann Simoneit, with the defenses based primarily on the III./GR 919 and 25 French tanks of Hptm. Wenk's Pz.-Abt. 206. The defenses to the west of the town were held by KG Hoffmann, which consisted mainly of the remains of Sturm-Abt. AOK 7 and GR 1058. To the east of the town was KG Rohrbach around St Floxel, while KG Müller covered the sector closer to the shore from Crisbecq up to Fontenay-sur-Mer.

By June 10, the 8th Infantry had reached its objective on the southwest outskirts of Montebourg, and, aside from some skirmishing on June 11, remained in a defensive posture until June 18.

The objective for the 12th Infantry was the Quinéville ridge, north of the Montebourg–Quinéville road. On June 10, the regiment pushed into the defenses of I./GR 922 of KG Rohrbach, with the town of Montebourg on its left flank. The outer perimeter of the town was heavily defended, and so the regiment made no effort to push into the town. On June 11, the regiment pushed up to its objective north of the highway, but in doing so, it lost contact with the other two regiments with Montebourg on its left flank, and the II./GR 920 of KG Rohrbach on its right. The divisional headquarters ordered it to pull back to a more defensible line along the Montebourg–St Floxel road.

At VII Corps headquarters, Collins wanted to establish the 4th Infantry Division on the Quinéville ridge until the Cotentin Peninsula had been cut off. Since the 22nd Infantry had taken such heavy losses in its prolonged fight for the Azeville and Marcouf batteries, he decided to reinforce the attack by adding the weight of another regiment, the experienced 39th Infantry from the newly arrived 9th Infantry Division. The plan was to launch the second phase of the push northward on June 12. The 39th Infantry was assigned to deal with remaining German coastal strongpoints, culminating in an assault against the concentration of German defenses around the town of Quinéville. This would free up the 22nd Infantry to push past Ozeville and reach its objectives north of the Montebourg–Quinéville road. In addition, Gen. Barton decided finally to attack the town of Montebourg itself using a task force under Lt. Col. Fred Steiner, the executive officer of the 8th Infantry, consisting of two infantry companies with engineer, artillery, and tank destroyer support.

Task Force Steiner set off for Montebourg on the morning of June 12, but it was far too weak to deal with the defenses in the town. The accompanying M10 tank destroyers came under heavy anti-tank gunfire, and the task force halted on the southern outskirts. General Barton was unwilling to risk heavy casualties by taking the town by storm, and so he ordered Steiner to pull back and patrol the outskirts.

Besides the gun bunkers, the MKB Marcouf site had an extensive array of other fortifications such as this R622 *Doppelgruppenunterstand*, a type of personnel bunker that could accommodate about 20 troops. It was protected by a Tobruk machine-gun pit at one end. The two completed gun bunkers can be seen on the horizon. (Author's photograph)

The 12th Infantry resumed its attack on the afternoon of June 12, advancing over the same terrain it had covered a few days before. The 2/12th Infantry encountered a few pillboxes near the quarry east of Les Fieffes-Dancel, and was counterattacked by a battle group of about 250 men, based around Alarmheiten Grabbe and the 709. Infanterie-Division divisional training company supported by a few French tanks. This counterattack was repulsed by the 2/12th Infantry. The advance by the 12th Infantry completely disrupted the defenses of KG Rohrbach, and Schlieben insisted that the battle group counterattack and regain its positions around St Floxel. The following morning, KG Rohrbach tried to stage another counterattack using elements of II./GR 919, I./GR 922, and II./GR 920, but the attack was a shambles and led to a general disintegration of the battle group.

The 22nd Infantry set off finally to overcome the defenses of the II./GR 922 in Ozeville. The fortified zone was supposed to be subjected to air attack, but when that did not materialize, the fortifications were bombarded for three hours with 2,000 rounds of 81mm mortar fire. The fighting for Ozeville came down to close-quarter bayonet fighting but, by the day's end, the 22nd Infantry had overcome the Ozeville defenses. The following day, the 22nd Infantry pushed up to the Quinéville ridge, but it took another day of fighting before it reached its final objectives. On June 14, the 3/22nd Infantry cleared the western suburbs of Quinéville.

The 39th Infantry saw its combat debut in Normandy on June 12. The 1st Battalion was assigned to cross the causeways over the inundated coastal zones and attack W14 from the rear. The 2nd Battalion was assigned to clear the MKB Marcouf fortified zone, though this took far less effort than expected since the garrison had withdrawn the night before. The 3rd Battalion pushed through the III./GR 922 defenses in Fontenay-sur-Mer. The following day, the 1st and 2nd Battalions continued the process of clearing the beach strongpoints, reaching the outskirts of StP 16 on June 13. That night, the garrison at StP 16, as well as the forces in W17 immediately to the north, were authorized to withdraw. The 3rd Battalion pushed northward against rearguards of KG Müller on June 13, and finally captured the town of Quinéville on June 14. This included the fortified 4. Batterie of HKAR 1261 as well as Oberst Triepel's "Ginsterhöhe" regimental artillery command bunkers, finally putting an end to German shelling of Utah Beach.

The 4th Infantry Division attacks on June 12–14 completely overcame the defenses of the two German battle groups east of Montebourg. The only thing that prevented a complete rout was the American decision to hold their position on the Quinéville Ridge over the next four days while awaiting the offensive farther south to cut off the Cotentin Peninsula. The lull was necessary owing to the heavy casualties suffered by the 4th Division in its first week of fighting. Kampfgruppe Rohrbach was a complete shambles, so Oberst Keil from GR 919 was brought in to reorganize the defenses. He convinced Schlieben that the forces in this sector were too weak to stage a counterattack, and so, instead, the focus was on establishing a new defense line from Montebourg to the Quinéville ridge. The newly arrived 77. Infanterie-Division was gradually integrated into the Montebourg defenses starting on June 14, but saw little combat for reasons that are explained below.

# CUTTING OFF THE COTENTIN

While the 4th Infantry Division continued to grind through the German defenses in front of Montebourg, Collins realized that the chances for a quick capture of Cherbourg had evaporated. Eisenhower's June 8 instructions to Collins to focus on the juncture of VII Corps and V Corps diverted him from the capture of Cherbourg. From Ultra decrypts of German Enigma radio communications, it was becoming obvious that the Germans were substantially reinforcing the Montebourg defenses from forces elsewhere in France, mainly from Brittany. Rather than depend on a single-division drive towards Cherbourg, on June 9 (D+3) Collins decided to cut off the Cotentin Peninsula to prevent further German reinforcements of the Cherbourg front prior to an eventual multi-division assault on the port.

Once the 82nd Airborne Division had finally consolidated its forces on both sides of the Mederet River, Collins gave the task of closing off the Cotentin to the newly arrived 90th Division. One of this division's regiments had already been assigned to the Montebourg front, so the attack westward towards the Douve River on June 10 began with its remaining two regiments.

The 357th Infantry moved over the La Fière bridge but ran into the defenses of GR 1057 past Le Motey. Inexperienced in bocage fighting, its lead battalion retreated into the positions of the 325th Glider Infantry. A second attack at dusk by another battalion was equally unsuccessful. Recognizing the weakness of the 91. Luftlande-Division in this sector, Marcks gradually reinforced the defenses with most of the remaining strength of the 243. Infanterie-Division, leaving only two infantry battalions and some of its artillery on the western Cotentin coast.

A squad from the 359th Infantry, 90th Division at the cafe in St Côme-du-Mont shortly after its arrival in Normandy on June 8, 1944. (NARA)

# Cutting off the Cotentin: June 10–18, 1944

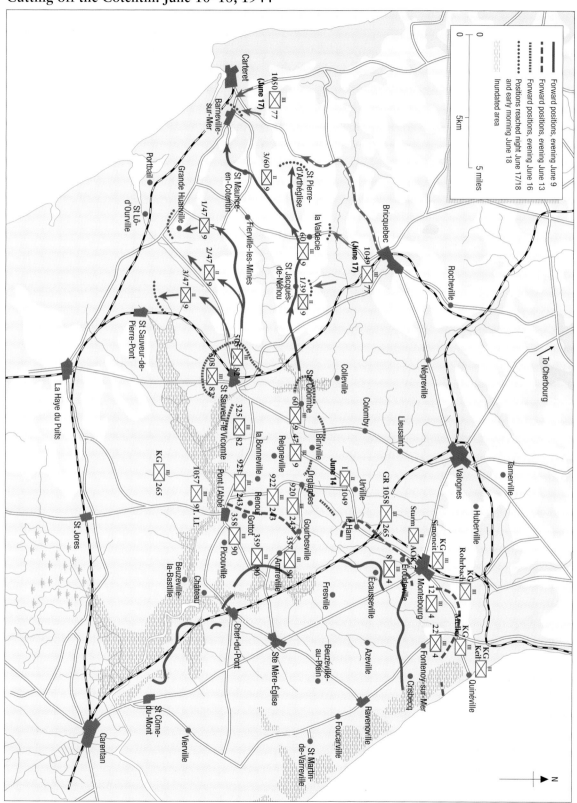

The 358th Infantry was assigned to reach Pont l'Abbé, and its lead battalion dug into defense positions short of the objective after having come under heavy fire. Grenadier-Regiment 1057 launched a counterattack in mid-afternoon, without success. The attacks continued the following day with 357th Infantry still unable to overcome the German defensive positions around Les Landes, and the 358th Infantry on the fringe of Pont l'Abbé. The following day, the 359th Infantry rejoined the division and reinforced the attack. The July 12 attack was further reinforced by the 746th Tank Battalion and additional artillery fire support. In spite of the reinforcements, the advance on June 12 and 13 was measured in mere hundreds of yards.

In frustration over the slow pace of the advance after four days of fighting, Collins visited the division on June 13. After reaching the divisional command post, Collins was aggravated when he could find no regimental or battalion headquarters, nor much evidence of fighting. Furious over the 90th Division's poor performance and inadequate leadership, Collins telephoned Bradley with plans to relieve the division's commander along with two regimental commanders. Owing to pressure to capture Cherbourg as quickly as possible, they decided to pull the 90th Division out of the line in favor of an experienced unit. Bradley agreed to the use of the 9th Infantry Division, regarded as being one of the best infantry divisions in theater.

The stalemate along the Montebourg front prompted Marcks' 84. AK headquarters to try to sort out the confused deployment that had been caused by the hasty injection of reinforcing units in the days after the Normandy landings. There was some concern that the Cherbourg front would become cut off, so a new command structure was installed, with Gruppe Hellmich taking over the control of the Cotentin defenses. Hellmich was the senior divisional commander in the sector, heading the 243. Infanterie-Division. This essentially served as corps headquarters controlling four divisions. However, Hellmich's headquarters did not have the communication resources to handle such a configuration, especially in light of frequent displacement of units.

Troops of the 9th Division pass through St Marie-du-Mont on June 13, 1944, in preparation for the start of the attack on June 14 to cut off the Cotentin Peninsula. (NARA)

The 709. Infanterie-Division was assigned the defense of the east side of the Montebourg defense line and the 77. Infanterie-Division to the center of the line starting to the west of Montebourg. The 243. Infanterie-Division held the front farther south, facing the 90th Infantry Division in the bocage country along the Douve River. Marcks was killed on June 12 when his staff car came under air attack near St Lô, and his place was taken temporarily by Gen. Wilhelm Fahrenbacher.

The substitution of the 9th Division for the failed 90th Division delayed the American advance for a day, so the attack resumed on June 14 with the 82nd Airborne Division on the left and the 9th Infantry Division on the right. These two divisions were opposed primarily by the battered 91. Luftlande-Division and elements of the 243. Infanterie-Division. The 82nd Airborne Division reached St Sauveur-le-Vicomte on the Douve River on June 16 while the 60th Infantry, 9th Division, reached the Douve River near Ste Colombe. With German resistance crumbling, Collins urged Eddy to push to the sea as rapidly as possible. During the night of June 16–17, a company from 3/60th Infantry riding on tanks and other armored vehicles reached the hill overlooking the coastal town of Barneville-sur-Mer before dawn. Early in the morning, the company advanced into the town, unoccupied except for a few startled German military policemen. The rapid advance by the 9th Division had severed the Cotentin Peninsula and cut off Cherbourg.

A GI of the 9th Division armed with a .45-cal. Thompson submachine gun crawls warily along the edge of a hedge near St Sauveur-le-Vicomte on June 16, 1944, during the fighting to cut off the Cotentin Peninsula. (NARA)

GIs of the 9th Division use a roadside drainage ditch for cover during a skirmish near St Sauveur-le-Vicomte on June 21, 1944. In the background to the right is their 1½-ton weapons carrier, while to the left is an abandoned German truck. (NARA)

## PANZERS REINFORCE THE MONTEBOURG FRONT, JUNE 9–10, 1944 (PP. 36–37)

There were only two Panzer units on the Cotentin Peninsula on D-Day, both replacement and training units (*Panzer-Ersatz-und-Ausbildung-Abteilungen*), equipped mainly with war-booty French tanks of the 1940 campaign. Panzer-Ersatz-und-Ausbildung-Abteilung 100 was headquartered at Château de Francquetot and included 17 Renault R-35s, eight Hotchkiss H-39s, one Somua S-35, one Char B1 bis, and one PzKpfw III. It was attached to the 91. Luftlande-Division on D-Day and saw extensive fighting with the 82nd Airborne Division along the Mederet River, most notably the battles for the La Fière bridge.

The other tank unit was Pz.-ers.u.ausb.Abt. 206, which was equipped with 20 Hotchkiss H-39s, ten Somua S-35s, two Renault R-35s, and six Char B1 bis. This battalion was originally stationed on the Jobourg Peninsula west of Cherbourg. German pre-invasion planning was concerned that the Allies might land on the Jobourg Peninsula as a means of quickly enveloping Cherbourg from the land side, and the area had an especially dense assortment of defenses. When US operational plans were discovered on June 8, it became clear that the Allies had no immediate intentions to land on the Jobourg Peninsula. As a result, units stationed there were free to be redeployed to more important sectors. General von Schlieben desperately wanted reinforcements for the Montebourg front and he was given permission to shift Panzer-Abt. 206 to this sector on June 9. It arrived there later in the day. Schlieben ordered the tanks to be driven to the outskirts of Montebourg at night in the hopes that

the sound of the tanks would alarm the Americans and bolster the morale of the German defenders. He later admitted, "Our infantrymen did not know that these vehicles were merely toys."

The most common tank in Pz.-Abt. 206 was the Hotchkiss H-39 (**1**), known in German service as the Panzerkampfwagen 38H 735(f). Most of these in the battalion were the late-production type, which had the improved SA.38 37mm gun with long barrel as well as other updates such as the unditching tail on the rear. German depot units modified the French tanks in several ways. The original French Hotchkiss lacked an opening turret cupola, using instead a closed dome for observation. German tactical doctrine favored the use of turret hatches to give the tank commander better situational awareness. As a result, the German depots cut off the tops of the French dome cupola, and replaced it with split hatches (**2**). The Hotchkiss retained the rear turret hatch, which allowed the commander to travel outside the vehicle while in transit (**3**). Another change to the German Hotchkiss tanks was the substitution of German tank radios.

The tank at the end of the column is a Somua S-35 cavalry tank (**4**), one of the best tanks of the French Army in 1940. These had many of the same modifications as the Hotchkiss and were more popular with German tank crews because of the greater interior hull volume and the better 47mm tank gun. Armor protection of both French tanks was good by 1940 standards, but vulnerable to all typical US Army anti-tank weapons of the 1944 period.

# PLAN HEINRICH

The renewal of the westward American offensive on June 14 provoked a major row among senior German leaders. Rommel had begun moving the 77. Infanterie-Division into the Cotentin Peninsula on June 9, but he was unwilling to sacrifice too many troops in a forlorn attempt to hold the Cotentin Peninsula and Cherbourg. Furthermore, assessments of the supply situation in Cherbourg indicated that it could not support much more than its usual ration strength of 25,000. Resupply of Cherbourg was unlikely and pushing too many forces into its perimeter would simply exhaust its supplies more quickly. Rommel was also concerned that, once the Americans reached the west coast of Cotentin, they were likely to proceed southward. This would allow them to push westward towards Brittany or eastward to undermine the defenses around St Lô.

With these factors in mind, on June 15 he ordered the amalgamation of the remnants of the 709. Infanterie-Division and 243. Infantry-Division into Kampfgruppe Schlieben with a mission to hold the Montebourg line and eventually fall back to defend the Cherbourg Landfront. The 77. Infanterie-Division was not yet fully committed to the Montebourg front and, along with the surviving elements of the 91. Luftlande-Division, was consolidated under Kampfgruppe Hellmich and instructed to prepare to withdraw to the southwest to create the new Westfront defense line to seal off the Cotentin Peninsula and shield Brittany and the St Lô front. On learning of this decision, Berlin initially refused permission for the withdrawal.

Because of the heavy losses suffered by the 22nd Infantry Regiment in its advance up the coast, Collins injected the experienced 39th Infantry of the newly arrived 9th Division to deal with the heavily fortified coastal town of Quinéville. Here, troops for the 39th Infantry advance through a shattered building on June 14. (NARA)

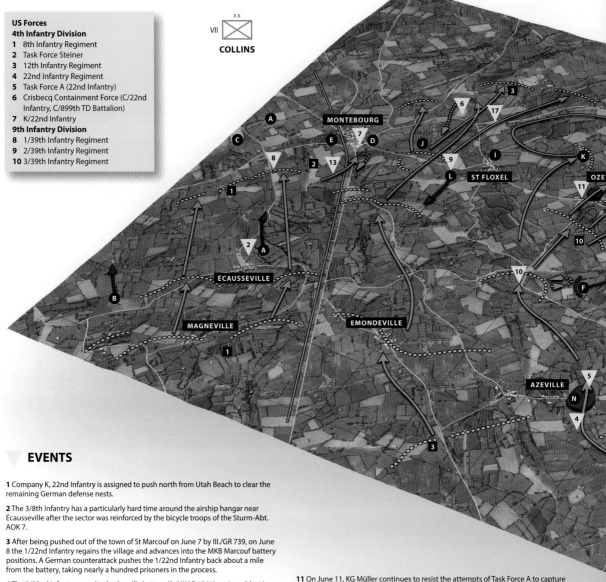

US Forces
**4th Infantry Division**
1 8th Infantry Regiment
2 Task Force Steiner
3 12th Infantry Regiment
4 22nd Infantry Regiment
5 Task Force A (22nd Infantry)
6 Crisbecq Containment Force (C/22nd Infantry, C/899th TD Battalion)
7 K/22nd Infantry
**9th Infantry Division**
8 1/39th Infantry Regiment
9 2/39th Infantry Regiment
10 3/39th Infantry Regiment

VII  XX  COLLINS

MONTEBOURG
ST FLOXEL
OZEV
ÉCAUSSEVILLE
MAGNEVILLE
EMONDEVILLE
AZEVILLE

## ▼ EVENTS

**1** Company K, 22nd Infantry is assigned to push north from Utah Beach to clear the remaining German defense nests.

**2** The 3/8th Infantry has a particularly hard time around the airship hangar near Écausseville after the sector was reinforced by the bicycle troops of the Sturm-Abt. AOK 7.

**3** After being pushed out of the town of St Marcouf on June 7 by III./GR 739, on June 8 the 1/22nd Infantry regains the village and advances into the MKB Marcouf battery positions. A German counterattack pushes the 1/22nd Infantry back about a mile from the battery, taking nearly a hundred prisoners in the process.

**4** The 2/22nd Infantry assaults the Azeville battery (2./HKAR 1261) on June 8 but is unable to overcome the defenses.

**5** The 3/22nd Infantry resumes the attack against the Azeville battery on June 9 with tank support. The battery is finally overwhelmed and surrenders.

**6** The 3/12th Infantry penetrates the KG Rohrbach defenses east of Montebourg on June 9.

**7** Montebourg is reinforced late on June 9, including the light tanks of Panzer-Abteilung 206.

**8** The 8th Infantry's attacks to the west of Montebourg on June 10 succeed in dislodging the newly arrived II./GR 921, which retreats after its commander is killed.

**9** General Barton is concerned that the 12th Infantry is too exposed, in view of the slow pace of the neighboring 22nd Infantry, and on June 11 he orders the regiment to withdraw to the hill between St Floxel and Montebourg until the 22nd Infantry secures its right flank. KG Rohrbach tries to stem the momentum of the 12th Infantry east of Montebourg by staging a counterattack on June 12 with the recently arrived Alarmheiten Grabbe, but this fails.

**10** At 1630hrs on June 10, Task Force A of the 22nd Infantry sets out for its initial objective of Ozeville, progressing as far as the Château de Fontenay where it is stopped by III./GR 922 backed by heavy artillery support.

**11** On June 11, KG Müller continues to resist the attempts of Task Force A to capture Ozeville, which is not secured until the afternoon of June 12.

**12** Running out of ammunition, MKB Marcouf receives permission to withdraw on June 11, and escapes under the cover of darkness that night.

**13** On June 12, Task Force Steiner from the 8th Infantry makes an attempt to penetrate into Montebourg but is quickly rebuffed. As a result, Barton decides to contain the town rather than waste troops in an urban battle.

**14** On June 12, 1/39th Infantry crosses the causeways over the inundated coastal zones and attacks defense nest W14 from the rear.

**15** The 2/39th Infantry occupies MKB Marcouf after the withdrawal of the survivors the night before and then pushes over the causeways to clear remaining defense nests, reaching the outskirts of StP 16 by June 13.

**16** The 3/39th Infantry pushes through the III./GR 922 defenses near Fontenay-sur-Mer on June 12 at the start of its drive towards Quinéville.

**17** On June 13, KG Rohrbach tries to stage another counterattack against the 12th Infantry using elements of II./GR 919, I./GR 922, and II./GR 920, but it is repulsed with heavy casualties.

**18** The 3/39th Infantry pushes northward against rearguards of KG Müller on June 13, and finally captures the town of Quinéville on June 14.

# THE BATTLE FOR MONTEBOURG, JUNE 8–14, 1944

**Note:** Gridlines are shown at intervals of 1km

xxx
84 ⊠
**MARCKS**

**GERMAN FORCES**
**Kampfgruppe Hoffman**
A  Sturm-Abteilung AOK 7
B  GR 1058
C  II./GR 921

**Kampfgruppe Simoneit**
D  III./GR 919
E  Pz.-Abt. 206 (June 9)

F  **Kampfgruppe Müller**
G  III./GR 739
H  III./GR 922

**Kampfgruppe Rohrbach**
I  II./GR 920
J  I./GR 922 (June 9)
K  II./GR 922
L  Alarmheiten Grabbe

**Kampfgruppe Keil**
M  II./GR 919

**Fortified positions**
N  2./HKAR 1261
O  MKB Marcouf
P  Defense nest W11
Q  Defense nest W12
R  Defense nest W13
S  Defense nest W14
T  Defense nest W14a
U  Defense nest StP 16
V  Defense nest W17
W  Defense nest StP 18
X  Defense nest W21

QUINÉVILLE

FONTENAY-
SUR-MER

ST MARCOUF

N

The capture of St Sauveur on June 16 prompted Rundstedt and Rommel to consider the immediate withdrawal of Kampfgruppe Schlieben back from Montebourg and into the Cherbourg Landfront defenses, called Plan Heinrich. Rommel and Rundstedt met with Hitler later on June 16 at the Führerhauptquartier Wolfsschlucht 2 (Wolf Canyon 2) in Margival, France to discuss the course of future operations in Normandy. There was little consensus at the meeting, with Hitler stubbornly forbidding any withdrawals anywhere, while Rundstedt and Rommel asked for more tactical flexibility. At 1100hrs, Hitler categorically forbade any withdrawal from the Montebourg line to Cherbourg. He initially insisted that the largest possible forces be committed to the defense of Festung Cherbourg. He was reminded of the inadequate supply situation in Cherbourg and by evening he finally agreed to allow the 77. Infanterie-Division and Kampfgruppe Hellmich to withdraw southward, starting on June 17, ostensibly to create a new defense line. A request to move elements of the 319. Infanterie-Division from the Channel Islands to the Cherbourg front was denied. The day-long command paralysis would have tragic consequences for the 77. Infanterie-Division.

When Montebourg was finally abandoned on the night of June 19–20, it was a smoldering ruin after days of bombing and artillery shelling. The Wehrmacht truck on the right was a war-booty British Morris C8 Quad left behind during the withdrawal of the British Expeditionary Force from Cherbourg in 1940. (NARA)

An M20 armored utility car of Co. A, 801st Tank Destroyer Battalion enters the southern approaches of Montebourg on June 21, 1944, shortly after the capture of the city. (NARA)

By the time that Hitler's authorization arrived, the 77. Infanterie-Division was no longer facing a simple withdrawal, but would have to retreat through areas held by American units. Many areas were still no man's land, but the 77. Infanterie-Division did not have the luxury of conducting extensive reconnaissance. The first unit to begin the withdrawal was GR 1049 which ran into 1/39th Infantry of the 9th Infantry Division on the morning of June 18 near St Jacques-de-Nehou and was stopped. Another motorized column struck the 60th Infantry and was decimated by artillery fire. An American officer counted one light tank, three motorcycles, 23 vehicles, 12 half-track prime movers, 28 horse-drawn wagons, 51 horses, and 12 artillery pieces in the first 5 miles of the road before being forced to halt by the density of the carnage on the road. The neighboring GR 1050 had more success, staging a bayonet charge to gain control of a bridge over the Ollande River near St Lô-d'Ourville from the hapless 357th Infantry of the 90th Division, capturing about a hundred GIs. About 1,300 men broke out before the gap was finally sealed. In the event, this was the only major group to escape the encirclement, and the 77. Infanterie-Division lost most of its artillery in the breakout attempt. Both Gen. Hellmich and the commander of the 77. Infanterie-Division, Gen. Rudolf Stegmann, were killed during the retreat on June 17.

In the early morning hours of June 17, Hitler again changed his mind and another dispatch was sent to Schlieben authorizing a fighting withdrawal into the Cherbourg Landfront defense line but reiterating his earlier injunction that Festung Cherbourg had to be "held at all costs."

# NORTH TO CHERBOURG

On June 18, 1944, Field Marshal Bernard Montgomery laid out the immediate tasks for the Allied forces in Normandy under his 21 Army Group command. Bradley's First US Army was to take Cherbourg while the British Second Army was to take Caen. The urgency of capturing Cherbourg became greater on the night of June 19–20 when a severe storm in the Channel demolished much of the Mulberry harbor that had been erected off Omaha Beach.

The breakthrough to the west Cotentin coast prompted Bradley to reorganize the forces on the Cotentin Peninsula. The new VIII Corps headquarters under Maj. Gen. Troy Middleton was given the 82nd Airborne and 90th Division with an assignment to defend towards the south and prevent any German forces from reinforcing the Cotentin Peninsula. Collins' VII Corps now consisted of three infantry divisions, the 4th, 9th, and 79th Divisions, which had the mission of advancing on Cherbourg. Eddy's 9th Division began a change in direction from west to north, moving against the

The fighting south of Cherbourg often took place in bocage country. This patrol from the 79th Division steps around debris left behind from a previous engagement. Several of the German units on the Cherbourg front were bicycle-mobile, accounting for the numerous bike frames seen here. (NARA)

western side of Cherbourg. Barton's 4th Division continued its push up along the eastern coast on the Montebourg–Valognes axis to Cherbourg, while the newly deployed 79th Division pushed up the center between the other two divisions. The 4th Cavalry Group was assigned to protect the flanks of the advance.

The drive on Cherbourg began in the pre-dawn hours of June 19 with the 4th Division starting at 0300hrs, followed by the 9th and 79th Divisions at 0500hrs. German defenses by this stage of the campaign were the disorganized remnants of four divisions. The 9th Division was facing portions of GR 920 and GR 921 from the 243. Infanterie-Division along with some bits of the 77. Infanterie-Division that had failed to escape southward during the breakout attempt two days before. The 79th Division in the center faced parts of the 77. Infanterie-Division as well as remnants of the 91. Luftlande-Division. The 4th Division was facing most of the 709. Infanterie-Division, the survivors of Sturm-Abt. AOK 7, and surviving parts of the 243. Infanterie-Division.

The initial attacks made steady progress as the German units tended to withdraw after first contact. Owing to the limited mobility of his forces, at noon on July 19, Gen. Schlieben ordered the disengagement of his forces from the Montebourg front, and withdrawal into the Cherbourg Landfront. The main retreat route along the Valognes–Cherbourg highway was protected by a rearguard from Pionier-Bataillon 709 and the tanks of Pz.-Abt. 206. The withdrawal proved to be less costly than expected, because the wet, cloudy weather prevented interference from Allied fighter-bombers.

The artillery duels between US and German forces around Montebourg forced many civilians to flee their homes. This scene took place on the road between Montebourg and Le Rôti on June 21, 1944. The wrecked 75mm Marder I belonged to Leutnant Max Ogroske's 1. Kompanie/ Panzerjäger-Abt. 709, which took heavy losses in the fighting from Ste Mère-Église to Montebourg. Ogroske was killed on June 12. (NARA)

# CHERBOURG LANDFRONT

Cherbourg is located in a shallow bowl surrounded by hills on all sides, making it very difficult to defend close to the port itself. As a result, as part of the Atlantikwall fortification program, a separate Cherbourg Landfront, known officially as KVU Cherbourg-Land, was built in 1943–44. This defensive line consisted of about 85 defense nests (*Widerstandsnesten*) in a hemispherical shape about 25km wide, 10km deep, and about 45km long (15 x 6 x 28 miles). These defense nests were built in a similar fashion to those on the coast and typically contained a gun casemate with an anti-tank gun or field gun, supported by Tobruks or other small defense positions with mortars and machine guns and extensive trenches. Besides the defense nests on the periphery, the interior zone had a significant number of Flak positions for city defense. The Cotentin Peninsula had also been selected as the site for V-1 cruise missile launch sites, and although most of these sites were not yet functional, they often had an assortment of concrete shelters and defenses that could form improvised defense works. On D-Day, the Landfront was manned at minimal levels by four battalions, two from the 243. Infanterie-Division, one from the 709. Infanterie-Division, and the fourth, a Georgian battalion.

The 79th Division history describes a typical Landfront defense nest:

> So-called pillboxes in the first line of German defenses which the 79th Division assaulted in the attack on Cherbourg were actually inland forts with steel and reinforced concrete walls 4 or 5ft thick. Built into the hills of Normandy so their parapets were level with surrounding ground, the forts were heavily armed with mortars, machine guns and 88mm rifles. Around the forts lay a pattern of smaller defenses, pillboxes, redoubts, rifle pits, sunken well-like mortar emplacements permitting 360 degree traverse, observation posts and other works to enable the defenders to deliver deadly cross-fire from all directions. Approaches were further protected by mine fields, barbed wire and anti-tank ditches at least 20ft wide at top and 20ft deep. Each strongpoint was connected to the other and all were linked to the mother fort by a system of

The eastern and western ends of the Cherbourg Landfront were anchored by heavily fortified strongpoints. This is the 40P8 armored cupola of a buried R644 bunker armed with two MG.34 machine guns and a 47mm anti-tank gun. This bunker covered the anti-tank ditch of defense nest W486 in Panzerwerk Westeck near Gréville. This bunker was protected to the higher "A" standard with walls 3.5m thick (11.5ft), making them resistant to almost any type of artillery. This photo was taken in February 1944 and shows the bunker with its full array of barbwire obstacles in front. (Library of Congress)

deep, camouflaged trenches and underground tunnels. The forts and pillboxes were fitted with periscopes. Telephones tied in all the defenses. Entrance to these forts was from the rear, below ground level, through double doors of steel armor plate which defending garrisons clamped shut behind them. The forts were electrically lighted and automatically ventilated.

The principal problem facing the defense of the Landfront was Berlin's refusal to permit a timely retreat by the remaining elements of the threadbare 709. Infanterie-Division. When the withdrawal finally began on June 19, the division was still in close contact with the advancing American divisions. The lack of transport for the division meant that the withdrawal was slow and time-consuming. By the time the troops reached the defensive perimeter, they were exhausted, and there was considerable shuffling around as units attempted to create some form of coherent organization amongst the scattered defense nests. Berlin looked at its maps of the defensive ring around Cherbourg and deluded themselves into thinking that it represented a formidable bastion. The Cherbourg garrison commander, Gen.Maj. Robert Sattler, later remarked that "a three year old boy does not grow a beard if you declare him a man, and a town does not become a fortress by being declared a fortress." Schlieben also complained that the troops had developed a "bunker psychosis." After having been pounded by American field artillery and naval gunfire for more than a week, some units hunkered down in the bunkers of the Landfront and showed little inclination towards aggressive patrolling. Schlieben organized the defense of the Landfront based on the four remaining regimental headquarters. From west to east, they were deployed as follows:

This is a view from the rear of an R634 bunker with 20P7 armored cupola showing the underground access trench. This bunker was part of Panzerwerk Osteck of Strongpoint 235 near Carneville to the east of Cherbourg. Besides the army defense nests, this strongpoint contained the Luftwaffe's Tausendfüssler (Millipede) radar complex of 12./Luft.Nachr.Rgt. 53. (NARA)

| Kampfgruppe Müller | GR 922 (243. ID) |
| Kampfgruppe Keil | GR 919 (709. ID) + MG-Btl. 17 |
| Kampfgruppe Köhn | GR 739 (709. ID) + Festungs-Stamm-Abt. 84 |
| Kampfgruppe Rohrbach | GR 729 (709. ID) + Ost-Btl. 549 |

These battle groups had a mixture of troops from various units, including some personnel from divisions that had withdrawn from the peninsula, such as the 77. Infanterie-Division and 91. Luftlande-Division. The regimental sectors were grossly overextended; the original plans expected the Landfront to be manned by three divisions, not four emaciated regiments. Oberst Köhn estimated the battalion strengths in his command to average about 70–180 men compared with a starting strength of about 800 men. On June 20–21, many of the regiments received hasty reinforcements from the city including Navy alarm units (*Marine Alarmheiten*), consisting of naval personnel organized into infantry. These naval units were usually deployed in company strength, but the army commanders soon despaired of their willingness to fight after many companies simply wandered back to the security of Cherbourg. The other source of reinforcement came from teenage German workers of the Reichsarbeitsdienst (RAD) who had been involved in the numerous construction projects around Cherbourg. These recruits were enthusiastic but not well trained. The unit commanders had a hard time integrating these naive youngsters with the weary, battle-shocked veterans who had been fighting continuously for more than a week. The last-minute infusion of these recruits brought many of the battalions close to paper strength, though in reality their combat value was low.

One of the more common weapons in the Cherbourg Landfront was this 50mm KwK *Behelfssockellafette*, a special pedestal-mounted version of the obsolete 50mm tank gun from the PzKpfw III tank. These were widely used in the Atlantikwall coastal defenses for anti-craft defense. This one was photographed after its capture by the 79th Division and was part of defense nest W449, part of Strongpoint Valogener-Strasse on the Valognes–Cherbourg highway. (NARA)

Troops of the 79th Division take a breather in one of the anti-tank ditches shielding the Cherbourg Landfront while other troops bring up boxes of K-rations. (NARA)

This 88mm Flak gun of Flak-Regiment 30 was part of a battery of four in defense nest W491 at La Guéretterie east of La Glacerie that was attacked on June 24 by the 2nd Battalion, 8th Infantry, supported by a platoon of tanks of the 70th Tank Battalion. The position also included a 37mm Flak gun and two 20mm Flak autocannons, reinforced by a battery of four 105mm field guns of Artillerie-Regiment 1709 that had withdrawn to this area. The site was overwhelmed after a day of fighting, and about 80 prisoners taken. The officers inspecting the gun are (left to right) the battalion commander, Lt. Col. Carlton MacNeely, the Co. K commander, Lt. John Rebarchek, and Capt. George Mabry, battalion S-3 (operations). Rebarchek was recommended for the Medal of Honor for his actions that day, later receiving the Distinguished Service Cross instead. (NARA)

Schlieben attempted to reinforce the front with Flak batteries from within the Cherbourg defenses, but this proved difficult because of a lack of prime movers. For the final defense of Cherbourg, the garrison had a ration strength of about 25,000 men, though many of these were tied down to the coastal defenses or were naval personnel assigned to the various port commands. Schlieben reported the Festung Cherbourg strength to be 21,000 men, of which 4,100 were naval personnel.

# BREACHING THE CHERBOURG LANDFRONT

The renewed VII Corps offensive on June 19 varied in pace from sector to sector. There were far more rearguard troops along the main route of Montebourg–Valognes–Cherbourg than in some of the more remote sectors. Montebourg had been abandoned by the Germans on the night of June 18, except for scattered rearguards, and was occupied by US troops by 1905hrs on June 19. The 4th and 79th Divisions reached the outskirts of the city of Valognes by the evening of June 19, but waited until June 20 to advance through the city because of the extensive destruction and rubble caused by aerial bombing and artillery shelling. All three American divisions reached the outer perimeter of the Cherbourg Landfront on June 20.

The strength of the Landfront defenses varied considerably because of the erratic dispositions of Schlieben's ragged forces. By the end of June 21, the 4th Infantry Division pushed through the KG Rohrbach Landfront defenses except along the main road into the eastern Cherbourg suburbs through the Bois du Coudray, the woods being blocked by a formidable line of defenses on the heights overlooking the Saire River. The other two US infantry divisions began probing the defenses only that day.

During the evening of June 21, VII Corps broadcast an ultimatum to the Cherbourg garrison, indicating that the city was surrounded and demanding surrender. There was no response by the time of the deadline on the morning of June 22. In reality, none was expected. In the event, Collins planned to stage major airstrikes in anticipation of an effort to break through the fortified Landfront on June 22. He coordinated an attack plan with Maj. Gen. Elwood Quesada, commander of IX Tactical Air Command. Allied fighter-bombers would conduct a series of strafing, rocket, and bomb attacks, followed by medium bomber attacks against 11 principal targets, mainly concentrations of fortifications along the main routes into Cherbourg as well as some of the principal Cherbourg defenses such as Fort du Roule.

Following preliminary artillery bombardments before noon on June 22, the 2nd Tactical Air Force (RAF) began the air assault with four squadrons of Typhoons and six squadrons of Mustangs starting at 1240hrs. Their primary objective was to suppress the German Flak positions around the city with rockets and machine-gun strafing. The flak over many sites was intense. Four Mustangs were shot down, as well as the Typhoon of Squadron Leader I. J. Davies, the

On June 22, the Ninth Air Force staged a series of raids on targets on the Cherbourg front. This is an A-20G Havoc medium bomber attacking a target on the Cherbourg Landfront. (NARA)

# North to Cherbourg: June 19–21, 1944

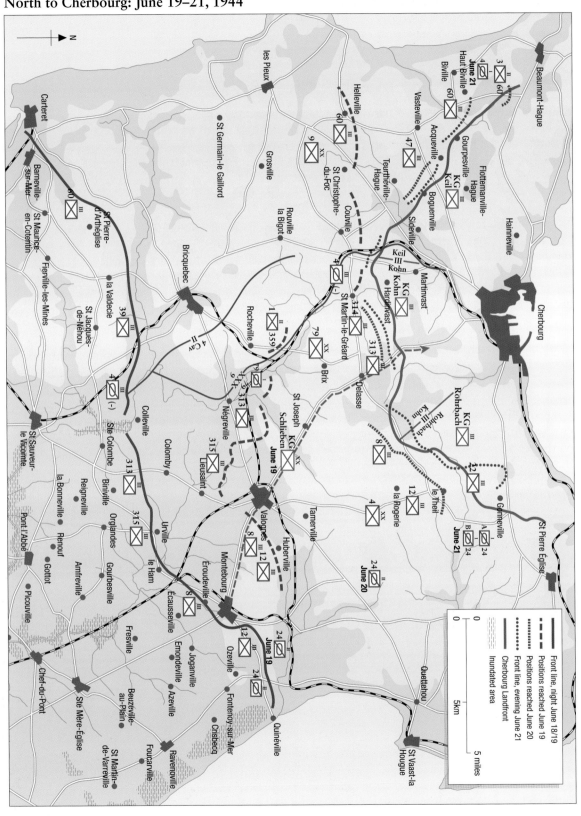

commander of 198 Squadron. At 1300hrs, the attack was taken over by 557 fighters of 12 fighter groups of the Ninth Air Force carrying 520 tons of 500-pound bombs; each P-51 and P-38 carried two and the P-47 carried three. At 1400hrs, medium bombers of IX Bomber Command began their attacks against the 11 main targets with 590 tons of bombs. The Germans claimed to have shot down 80 Allied aircraft. While not that severe, losses were still significant: 24 fighters and 12 bombers lost, four fighters and one bomber damaged beyond repair, and 42 fighters and 90 bombers damaged.

The airstrikes had disappointing results. The initial assessment was that four of the targets had been well hit, but seven not seriously damaged. It was not appreciated at the time, but all of the major bunkers along the front were invulnerable to 500-pound bombs; only the small Tobruk gun pits and trenches were vulnerable. The fighter squadrons were operating mainly from England, and it proved difficult for many pilots to become oriented over the target area, with some strikes being conducted against US Army positions. The attacks were more effective in some sectors, with the 9th Division getting the best results by suppressing known German Flak positions with divisional artillery before the airstrikes. When the infantry regiments started their attack in mid-afternoon, the forward German defense line had not been appreciably damaged, though the attacks had further demoralized the already shaky defenders.

The 9th Infantry Division was facing Kampfgruppe Keil to the southwest of Cherbourg. Kampfgruppe Keil consisted of two battalions of GR 919 and MG-Bataillon 17 on a front about 8km (5 miles) wide with each of the battalions deployed in six to seven defense nests. On June 22, the 9th Infantry Division pushed through several weak points in the defense line, capturing several defense nests in the afternoon and evening. Keil decided to commit his modest reserve, a *Fallschirmjäger* training company and a Georgian company, on the morning of June 23 along the boundary line between MG-Btl. 17 and III./GR 919 to recover several of the captured defense nests. Although the units made progress at first, they ran into the 39th Infantry, which was cleaning up defense nests that had been bypassed the previous day. The German counterattack was repulsed. The 60th Infantry made deep inroads near Flottemanville-Hague on June 23 into the sector held by III./GR 919, forcing Keil to scrape the barrel for units to try to stem the breakthrough. A few tanks from the Pz.-Abt. 206, the regimental supply company, and an anti-aircraft machine-gun platoon from II./GR 919 were

GIs of the 313th Infantry, 79th Division pose In front of a 20P7 6-Schartenturm armored cupola, the only visible sign of the large R634 bunker buried underneath. This was part of defense nest W449 in the hamlet of La Devise, part of the Valognes road strongpoint (StP Valogener-Strasse) near the main RN13 Valognes–Cherbourg highway. This strongpoint was overrun by the 79th Division on June 23. (NARA)

deployed on Hill 179, halting the 60th Infantry around nightfall. By then, the III./GR 919 sector had been completely penetrated and the battalion staff surrounded. The 47th Infantry penetrated the defenses of MG-Btl.17 on the eastern flank of KG Keil, pushing beyond the Mont du Roc woods. By the end of June 23, the 9th Infantry Division had penetrated a few kilometers past the crust of the Landfront and was about 5km (3 miles) from the outskirts of Cherbourg.

The 9th Infantry Division continued its drive to the northeast on June 24, leaving the 60th Infantry on its left flank to deal with remnants of KG Keil. The 47th Infantry advanced on the left and the 39th Infantry on the right, pushing through the remnants of MG-Btl. 17 and III./GR 919. With the KG Keil sector completely overrun and its remaining units in retreat towards Cherbourg, Schlieben realized that the US Army would soon reach the sea to the west of Cherbourg. Berlin had made it clear that it wanted the Jobourg Peninsula to be held to the last, and this would be the final opportunity to reinforce the western sector. Kampfgruppe Müller on the far western side of the Landfront had not been reached by American forces, so Schlieben ordered the regiment to withdraw units east of the Landfront on the night of June 24–25 along the coast road and to reorient the defenses. The Landfront defenses in this sector faced westward and away from the city; the American attack was most likely to come from inside the Landfront towards the east. Schlieben wanted the defenses led by an able commander, and instructed Keil to take over command. The force on the Jobourg Peninsula was renamed KG Keil, but, aside from the command staff, it was a completely different unit from the battle group which had fought along the Landfront on June 22–24.

The attack on June 22 by the 79th Division in the center of the American advance had focused on Kampfgruppe Köhn, consisting primarily of elements of GR 739, reinforced with a fortification battalion from the city and improvised alarm units. The main Valogne–Cherbourg highway passed through the center of this sector, and this was the focal point of the American attack. Owing to its obvious importance, the highway was one of the strongest points on the Landfront, with defense nests in depth along the road. A cluster of German defenses near the highway at Les Chèvres consisted of three strongpoints: StP La Vaquerie (three defense nests) on the west side of the road, StP Valogener-Strasse (six defense nests) astride the highway, and StP La Réveillerie (three defense nests) on the east side of the road. This site had been bombed and strafed by Allied fighter-bombers during the June

The main Wehrmacht communication center for the Landfront was located in this large bunker to the east of the Valognes–Cherbourg highway near La Mer à Canards. It was inadvertently bypassed by the 314th Infantry, 79th Division during the advance on June 24 and continued to broadcast information back to Cherbourg. When it was discovered later, this platoon was sent to demolish it. Two soldiers are walking away from the entrance after having placed explosive charges inside that were detonated moments after this photo was taken. (NARA)

22 raids. It was attacked by the 313th Infantry on July 23, with one battalion heading directly up the road and the other two attempting to outflank it. After heavy fighting, this series of strongpoints was cleared by the end of the day.

The 313th Infantry continued up the road to the next defense site on the highway near La Mare à Canards. This strongpoint began with defense nest W548 with two anti-tank gun bunkers near Crossroads 177/La Banque à Genets, while farther up the road was a fortified 88mm Flak battery of 4./gem.Flak-Abt. 152 (o) in W521 at Les Rouges Terres. In addition, there was another defense nest, W522 immediately north near La Glacerie. The 313th Infantry advance had been so quick that Allied fighter-bomber units had not been properly briefed on their location. They were inadvertently hit by US fighter-bombers in the late afternoon and the attack stalled. Owing to the heavy casualties suffered by the 313th Infantry on June 23, the 314th Infantry took the lead when the attack resumed on the morning of June 24. The defenses along the highway were overcome by late morning. The 79th Division continued to advance towards Cherbourg in the afternoon, but was eventually halted by heavy fire from the Octeville suburbs. By this stage, the 9th and 79th divisions had pulled alongside one another a short distance from the outer Cherbourg suburbs.

The 4th Division had already penetrated the Landfront defenses in its sector prior to the June 22 airstrikes. The most pressing issue was to clear the Landfront defenses on the west side of the Bois du Coudray that had stymied the advance of the 12th Infantry the day before. This was accomplished on June 23, with two battalions reaching Crossroad 140 by the afternoon.

French civilians wave, as a column from the 4th Infantry Division advances along the Montebourg–Valognes road on June 23, 1944. The M3A1 half-track is named "Dirty Gertie" and is followed by an M4A1 Duplex Drive amphibious tank of the 70th Tank Battalion. (NARA)

## AIR STRIKE ON CHERBOURG DEFENSES, JUNE 22, 1944 (PP. 54–55)

On June 22, 1944, the Ninth Air Force conducted a massive series of bombing raids in the Cherbourg area, trying to soften up German defenses in preparation for the ground offensive. This scene shows the strike by B-26C Marauder bombers (1) of the 555th Bomb Squadron, 386th Bomb Group, based at the time at Great Dunmow, Essex. The B-26 could carry a maximum of 5,800 pounds of bombs, though typical loads were less.

The attack began with preliminary strikes by RAF 2nd Tactical Air Force fighters and Ninth Air Force P-47 Thunderbolt fighter-bombers. The bomber mission was flown by 396 A-20 and B-26 medium bombers of all 11 bomb groups of IX Bomber Command. The bomber strikes were conducted starting at 1400hrs, about an hour before the ground attack by Collins' VII Corps. The missions started at the southern end of the bomb zone and moved northward using 590 tons of bombs. Collins had requested the "air pulverization" of 11 main targets. Losses were 12 bombers lost, 1 bomber damaged beyond repair and 90 bombers damaged. Later in the day, the B-26s struck again, hitting marshalling yards, German headquarters, and fuel dumps.

Later assessments of the bombing mission concluded that the attacks had a demoralizing effect on German troops in the bomb zone, but actual damage to the fortified structures of the Cherbourg Landfront had been disappointing. After the fighting, USAAF teams were sent to assess the level of damage. For example, the attack on Fort du Roule had involved 37 B-26 bombers dropping 177 500-pound General Purpose (high explosive-fragmentation) bombs. The analysis concluded: "The accuracy of the bombing was good but the relatively small sized GP bombs did very little demolition in the fort except where some prefabricated wooden personnel buildings were demolished. Some of the outer walls of part of the fort on top of the hill were destroyed. The bombing had a tremendous effect on the morale of the personnel within the fort. However, in the subterranean tunnels housing the guns which were firing into the city of Cherbourg no damage resulted from the bombing attack."

One discovery by the teams was that the decision to use delayed fusing, 0.1 second for the nose fuse and .01 seconds for the tail fuse, proved very effective when bombing non-hardened targets such as entrenchments. However, such fusing proved ineffective against steel-reinforced bunkers. When the bombs struck the reinforced concrete, the steel casings broke apart before the fuses detonated the high explosive content, leading to low-order detonation.

Isolated German units flowing back towards Cherbourg continued to threaten the regiment's supply lines and led to several skirmishes in the rear areas. Likewise, the 22nd Infantry on the division's far right continued to fight isolated skirmishes with German troops moving back towards Cherbourg as well as organized counterattacks from the heavily defended Flugplatz-Théville airbase. The German *Kampfgruppe* commander, Oberst Rohrbach, was captured during the June 23 fighting. On the left flank, the 8th Infantry made modest gains in its advance towards La Glacerie and the Trotebec River. The area immediately behind the Landfront had a secondary line made up of a cluster of three Luftwaffe fortified Flak positions and a V-1 cruise missile site. The 2/8th Infantry reached the outskirts of La Glacerie only on June 24.

As VII Corps began reaching the outer suburbs of Cherbourg on June 24, Collins began to outline the final plans for the assault. Some radio traffic was intercepted concerning reinforcement of the Jobourg Peninsula, and there was some concern that the Germans might pull some units out of Cherbourg to reinforce the peninsula. As a result, Collins instructed Eddy's 9th Division to reach the sea to the west of the port, thereby cutting off any possible reinforcements. The assignment was handed to the 60th Infantry, but in reality, KG Müller had already moved its forces into the peninsula and Schlieben had no intention of weakening the defenses of Festung Cherbourg any further. The VII Corps plans for June 25 placed the emphasis of the assault on the city with the 9th and 79th divisions. The 9th Division was assigned to push into the western side of the city through the suburb of Octeville. The 79th Division was assigned to attack into Cherbourg by first overcoming the fortified hill occupied by Fort du Roule. The 4th Division, battered after two weeks of costly fighting, was given the secondary role of taking the eastern Tourville suburb.

A rifle squad advances towards Cherbourg during the fighting on June 25. (NARA)

# FESTUNG CHERBOURG

Although Schlieben was in command of the field units defending the Cherbourg Landfront, the command of the city was under Gen.Maj. Robert Sattler. With the Landfront defense ring breached on June 22–23, German troops were streaming into the city. On June 22, Hitler sent a personal message to Schlieben invoking Gneisenau's miraculous defense of Kolberg during the Napoleonic Wars. The following day, Hitler consolidated the command structure by appointing Schlieben as the commander of Festung Cherbourg; Sattler became his deputy. Some senior German commanders in Berlin were under the impression that the garrison could hold out for months because of the geography and the extensive fortifications around the port. Schlieben insisted on more reinforcements and supplies if Berlin expected the city to hold out.

There had been a modest stream of supplies brought in by the Kriegsmarine using S-boats and other craft. The Luftwaffe had attempted to airdrop supplies and conducted 107 sorties from June 20 to June 30. Some 188 tons of supplies had been dropped, mostly at night. Only a small fraction were collected by the Cherbourg garrison; some were dropped as far away as the Channel Islands. There were some discussions about reinforcing the Cherbourg garrison using heavy gliders to bring in supplies and troops, but the Luftwaffe knew that daylight missions would be suicidal and the issue was dropped. Fallschirmjäger-Regiment 15 in St Malo was alerted on June 23 to prepare for an airdrop into Festung Cherbourg but the mission was squashed later in the day by the OKW in Berlin, which was coming to realize that the situation in Cherbourg was hopeless. On the night of June 23–24, remaining Kriegsmarine craft left Cherbourg for other ports, the harbor was officially closed, and port demolition work began.

Forward artillery observers from the 4th, 9th, and 79th Infantry Divisions converged on the hills overlooking Cherbourg on June 25 to plan their artillery fire support missions. By this stage, the arsenal had already been set ablaze and can be seen burning on the left side of the picture. (NARA)

# Festung Cherbourg

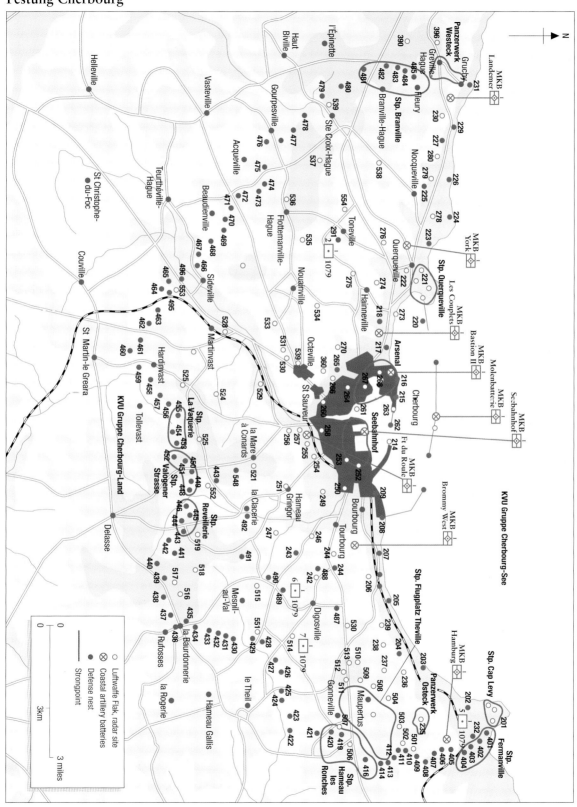

Two riflemen of the 39th Infantry, 9th Division, in the outskirts of Cherbourg during the fighting on June 26. On the helmet side is the "Triple A Bar None" insignia adopted by the unit commander, Col. Paddy Flint, which was an abbreviation of the unit slogan "Anything, Anywhere, Anytime, Bar Nothing." (NARA)

A 155mm M1 howitzer in full recoil during a fire mission on June 24. It belonged to the 312th Field Artillery Battalion, the heavy battalion of the 79th Division. (NARA)

With the outer crust of the Landfront comprehensively penetrated, there were no other significant defense lines guarding the city. In the wake of the 1898 Fashoda incident with Britain, the French had created a modest network of a half-dozen forts on the periphery of the city. The most important of these was Fort du Roule on the rocky hill overlooking the port. The other forts had been adapted by German occupation forces, mainly as Luftwaffe Flak sites. Besides these forts, the Luftwaffe had ringed the city with light and heavy Flak positions, and these often formed the center of German resistance efforts over the next few days of fighting on the outskirts of the city.

Fort du Roule was built on a rocky outcrop 117m high (38ft), on the southern side of the city. As the dominating point over the port, the hill had been fortified over the centuries. There was a 19th-century French fort on the crest of the hill, and Organization Todt had substantially reinforced the defenses in 1942–44 with an elaborate set of gun casemates and other defenses carved into the cliff-face, designated as Stützpunkt 255 (Strongpoint 255). There were four R671 gun casemates on the north side of the fort overlooking the port, armed with 105mm SKC/32U naval guns. The southern side of the fort was protected by an anti-tank ditch, trench lines, and a series of machine-gun bunkers to prevent approach from the landward side. The French Navy had used the mountain to create a set of underground chambers for storage and repair. In 1944, the tunnels were used for Kriegsmarine torpedo stowage and as workshops. The old French fort on top of the hill was also used as headquarters for two of the battalion headquarters of Flak-Regiment 30: Schwere-Abteilung 298(v) and gem.Flak-Abt. 152(v); the last provided the crews for the 37mm Flak guns mounted in the upper works of the fort.

By the evening of June 24, it was obvious that fighting would soon envelop the city. At dawn on June 25, a German medical officer accompanied by a captured American pilot came out of Cherbourg under a flag of truce to ask that the naval hospital be spared from shelling and for a supply of plasma. The plasma was provided, and it was accompanied by another surrender demand. By the time the surrender demand had reached Schlieben, the 314th Infantry, 79th Division was already assaulting Fort du Roule.

# THE BATTLE FOR FORT DU ROULE

The attack against Fort du Roule began at 0800hrs on July 25 with a squadron of P-47 Thunderbolts bombing the fort. Many of the bombs overshot their target and the damage was inflicted mainly on the Flak pits located around the top of the old French fort. This was followed by an assault by the 3/314th Infantry, which attempted to overcome the defensive belt on the southern side. The battalion methodically attacked the bunkers with machine-gun fire and mortars, finally advancing to the outer perimeter of the defenses. At this point, the attack was taken over by the fresh 2/314th Infantry. This battalion was equipped with Bangalore torpedoes, a type of explosive-filled pipe used by engineers for demolishing barbwire obstructions. The assault teams were also supplied with pole charges, a 15-pound block of explosives attached to a 10ft pole for attacking the embrasures of pillboxes.

After working their way through the barbwire obstructions, one of the platoons from Co. E became pinned down by one of the machine-gun bunkers. Corporal John Kelly volunteered to attack it with a pole charge. He approached the bunker under heavy fire, but the charge failed to silence the bunker, which was protected with a steel plate in the embrasure. He returned for a second charge, which damaged the machine-gun barrels of the embrasure. He returned for a third charge, which did enough damage to make the bunker vulnerable to grenade attack. After hurling grenades inside, the surviving German crew surrendered. Kelly was later awarded the Medal of Honor for this action. Once the bunkers south of the fort had been overcome, the 2/314th Infantry fought its way along the ridge on the northeast side of the fort.

While 2/314th Infantry fought its way along the western ridge of the fort, the 3/314th began to move along the eastern side of the fort. Besides receiving fire from the fort itself, the approach route was visible to the Flak battery located to the northeast of Octeville, 9./gem.Flak-Abt.152(o), equipped with

Fort du Roule sat on a rocky hill overlooking Cherbourg with the railway marshalling yards on its western side as seen here. During the attack by the 314th Infantry on June 25, the 2/314th Infantry approached the fort from the high ground behind it to the extreme upper right. The 3/314th Infantry advanced into the city at the base of the hill along Rue de Paris, evident from the buildings to the right. (NARA)

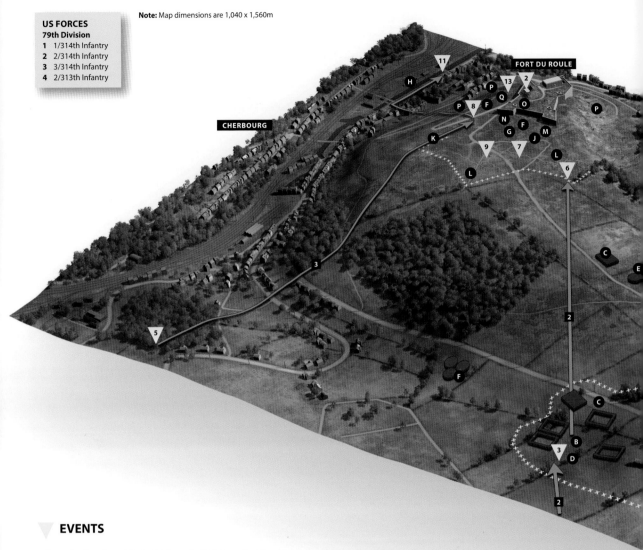

US FORCES
**79th Division**
1  1/314th Infantry
2  2/314th Infantry
3  3/314th Infantry
4  2/313th Infantry

**Note:** Map dimensions are 1,040 x 1,560m

FORT DU ROULE

CHERBOURG

## ▼ EVENTS

**1** The two lead battalions of the 314th Infantry, 2nd Battalion on the left and 3rd Battalion on the right, advance to a ridge line south of W251 by noon on June 24, but are stopped by heavy artillery fire and concentrated 37mm autocannon fire.

**2** A squadron of P-47 Thunderbolt fighter-bombers strafes and bombs Fort du Roule at 0800hrs, June 25.

**3** The 2/314th Infantry leaves the line of departure at 0830hrs on June 25 and captures the western side of "Point 46," the Ferme de la Montagne manor farm that includes the battery motor pool and barracks.

**4** The 1/314th Infantry captures the eastern side of the farm with the German Flak battery headquarters and is ordered to consolidate there around 1000hrs.

**5** An attempt by 3/314th Infantry to attack Fort du Roule direct is halted by heavy automatic weapons fire from the Flak battery on the ridge overlooking the stream and its associated fighting positions. This position was reduced by machine-gun and mortar fire.

**6** At 1000hrs, 2/314th Infantry sets out for Fort du Roule with Co. E in the lead, supported by Co. F. The two companies encounter the array of pillboxes on the southern edge of the fort, and Cpl. John Kelly manages to knock out one of the R630 machine-gun bunkers after three attempts using a pole charge with 15 pounds of TNT. Kelly was later awarded the Medal of Honor for this action.

**7** By 1145hrs, the bunkers on the southern side of the fort are overcome with about 100–150 German troops surrendering. The 2/314th Infantry is frustrated in its attempts to advance into the fort itself by the high walls and continuous fire from German positions along the wall.

**8** With the German defenses south of the fort under attack, the 3/314th Infantry advances to the western side of the fort. The acting commander of Co. K, Lt. Carlos Ogden, works his way to the edge of the fort with a grenade launcher attached to his rifle and a satchel of hand grenades. He knocks out one of the 37mm guns with a rifle grenade, and disables two Tobruk machine-gun pits. Ogden was later awarded the Medal of Honor for his actions that day.

**9** Both battalions eventually gain access into the fort itself later in the day and begin clearing the bunkers and buildings. The last of the buildings surrender at 2148hrs.

**10** The 2/313th Infantry advances from Hameau Gringor around 1400hrs and sends patrols into the southeastern outskirts of the city past the quarry and the Usine de Maupas factory. These patrols are fired on by the 105mm guns of MKB Fort du Roule in the casemates on the cliffs of Fort du Roule.

**11** On the morning of June 26, the 3/314th Infantry advances into Cherbourg along the western side of Fort du Roule and reaches the waterfront by late afternoon.

**12** While the 3/314th Infantry advances on the western side of the fort, the 1/314th moves from the Ferme de la Montagne and advances into Cherbourg along the eastern side of the fort.

**13** The 2/314th Infantry is assigned to complete the capture of the lower galleries of Fort du Roule. The casemates on the cliff are attacked using explosive charges delivered over the cliff-face using ropes and down ventilation shafts. The gun batteries remain active through the early evening, and do not surrender until 1900hrs. Eventually about 500 German troops surrender from the gun batteries and the storage tunnels at the base of the mountain.

# THE BATTLE FOR FORT DU ROULE, JUNE 25–26, 1944

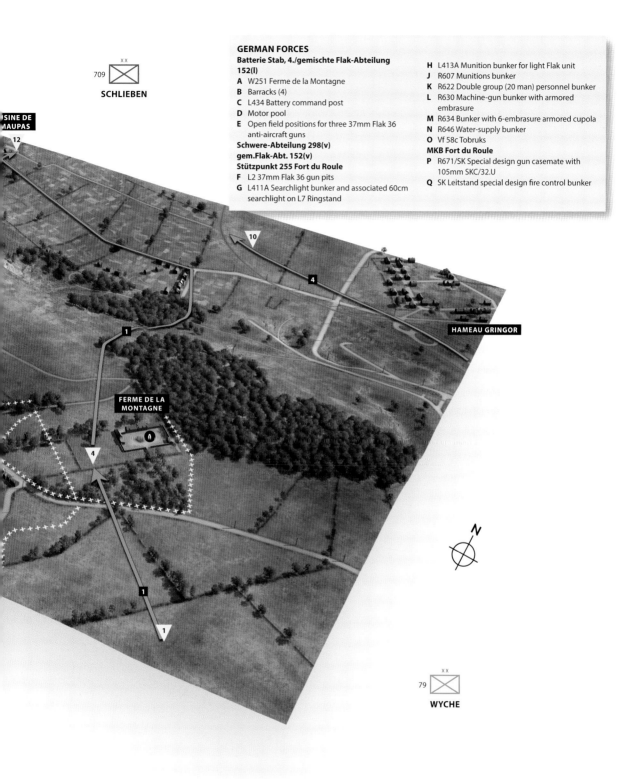

**GERMAN FORCES**

**Batterie Stab, 4./gemischte Flak-Abteilung 152(I)**
A  W251 Ferme de la Montagne
B  Barracks (4)
C  L434 Battery command post
D  Motor pool
E  Open field positions for three 37mm Flak 36 anti-aircraft guns

**Schwere-Abteilung 298(v)**
**gem.Flak-Abt. 152(v)**

**Stützpunkt 255 Fort du Roule**
F  L2 37mm Flak 36 gun pits
G  L411A Searchlight bunker and associated 60cm searchlight on L7 Ringstand

H  L413A Munition bunker for light Flak unit
J  R607 Munitions bunker
K  R622 Double group (20 man) personnel bunker
L  R630 Machine-gun bunker with armored embrasure
M  R634 Bunker with 6-embrasure armored cupola
N  R646 Water-supply bunker
O  Vf 58c Tobruks

**MKB Fort du Roule**
P  R671/SK Special design gun casemate with 105mm SKC/32.U
Q  SK Leitstand special design fire control bunker

pedestal-mounted 15mm automatic cannon. Company K was halted by a fortified area covered by gun and machine-gun fire. The acting company commander, Lt. Carlos Ogden, worked his way up the slope with a grenade launcher attached to his rifle and a satchel of hand grenades. He knocked out one of the guns with a rifle grenade, and disabled two Tobruk machine-gun pits. Ogden was later awarded the Medal of Honor for his actions that day. Ogden's initiative opened up the upper galleries of the fort, which were then methodically attacked by the two infantry battalions over the course of the day. The upper portions of the fort contained a significant number of buildings and gun pits that had to be cleared.

**ABOVE RIGHT**
This is a view of Fort du Roule looking to the northeast over the harbor with the inner and outer breakwaters evident. The 2/314th Infantry approached the fort from the Montagne du Roule to the fort's rear on the extreme right side of this photo. (NARA)

**ABOVE LEFT**
This photo was taken in February 1944 during the construction of StP 255 on the cliff-face below Fort du Roule. This is the R671 bunker at the western end of the strongpoint before its 105mm gun was installed. (NARA)

**RIGHT**
This view of Fort du Roule is looking southward and shows the forward face of the hill overlooking the city, which included Strongpoint 255 on the cliff below the fort. The triangles identify the bunkers built into the cliff consisting of four R671 gun casemates armed with 105mm SKC/32.U U-boat guns; the center triangle points to the fire control bunker. (NARA)

A rifle platoon of the 314th Infantry, 79th Division warily advances down the Avenue de Paris at the base of Fort du Roule during the fighting on June 25, 1944. (NARA)

While the 314th Infantry was fighting on top of Fort du Roule, the 2/313th Infantry had fought its way along the base of the hill and tried to advance into the city itself. It received heavy fire from the four gun casemates on the lower levels of Fort du Roule and was unable to advance further into the city. The lower galleries were not overcome until the following day.

In the 9th Division sector to the west, the 60th Infantry screened the left flank of the division while the 39th and 47th infantry regiments headed into the western suburbs of Cherbourg. Several of the forts built in 1898–1902 were in this sector, and these were used by German units as the focal points of their defense efforts. The 2/39th Infantry was held up for most of the day trying to blast out the 37mm Flak guns of 1./le.Flak-Abt. 931(v) which were ensconced around the Redoute des Fourches, blocking the road northwest of Octeville. Closer to the coast, the 47th Infantry collided with the Fort des Couplets outside Équeurdreville. The original French fort had been used as the basis for the fortified gun battery of the 8./HKAR 1261. Although

Troops of the 314th Infantry occupy a German trench line on the south side of Fort du Roule's Strongpoint 255. The R630 machine-gun bunker seen in the background was probably the one knocked out by Cpl. John Kelly in his Medal of Honor action. The 314th Infantry fought across this defense nest in the initial fighting for Fort du Roule on the morning of June 25 before reaching the fort itself. (NARA)

well fortified from the sea, it was weakly protected from landward except for an old moat. Preliminary bombardment by tank destroyers and artillery reduced the resolve of the 89 men of the gun battery and they surrendered within 15 minutes of the start of the infantry attack. Company F, 47th Infantry overcame modest resistance in the old Redoute du Tôt on the southwest extremities of Équeurdreville. This company reached the sea late in the day near the western side of the Arsenal Maritime, but pulled back before nightfall. As darkness fell, the city glowed from the fires that the Germans had set in the port facilities as the final stage of the destruction of the port.

# DEMOLITION OF THE PORT

Schlieben had argued as early as May 1944 that the port of Cherbourg should be demolished to reduce its value to the Allies. This had been strongly resisted by the Kriegsmarine, which intended to use the port for operations against the Allied invasion fleet in the Seine Bay. The Kriegsmarine attempted to reinforce the base on the night of June 8–9 with a destroyer flotilla but failed. In the face of strong Allied naval counter-actions, Konteradmiral Hennecke had to face the inevitable and withdrew the surviving S-boats to Le Havre on June 12. Permission to demolish the port was still not granted by Berlin, though the harbor commander, Fregattenkapitän Witt, had already begun preparations after extensive discussions with Schlieben and Hennecke. On June 23, Hitler had sent Schlieben explicit instructions that "if worst comes to worst, Cherbourg must fall into enemy hands only as a heap of ruins." When the last serviceable vessels left the port on the night of June 23–24, the time for demolition work had come.

A major from the 314th Infantry stands in one of the entrenchments on the Montagne du Roule to the east of Fort du Roule, with the fort evident to the left. The large fire evident in the background is from the naval arsenal on the western side of the city, which burned for several days. (NARA)

The demolitions focused on the port area. The famous railroad passenger terminal, the Gare Maritime, was severely damaged by the demolition of its main pillars and the detonation of a freight train full of explosives inside; all of its major components including the electrical generation plants and control systems were smashed. The neighboring Darse Transatlantique basin was ruined by the detonation of explosive charges on the neighboring

Major-General Collins, VII Corps commander, receives a briefing on the capture of Fort du Roule on June 26 from Capt. Robert Kirkpatrick of the 314th Infantry, 79th Division while standing on the easternmost of the casemates overlooking the city. (NARA)

piers to clog the passage with collapsed masonry. Five of the nine unloading cranes on the Quai de France were dropped on to the Gare Maritime and two of the remainder were partially toppled. The navy arsenal on the west side of the harbor was set ablaze and major structures such as the bridges and dry-dock gate were demolished. The fires in the harbor area were so intense that they continued to blaze for four days after the capture of the city. The outer breakwaters sheltering the Petite Rade artificial harbor were breached in numerous locations by explosions. The Quai Homet was cratered in nine locations while the Digue de Homet breakwater was blasted open to the sea. More than 100 ships, barges, cranes, and other obstructions were sunk throughout the port area to block the passages and basin entrances. The harbor minefields were substantially reinforced with more than 200 controlled mines, influence mines, moored mines, and the new KMA anti-craft mines. Indeed, Hitler was so pleased with the work of the Kriegsmarine in demolishing the harbor that he awarded the Knight's Cross to Konteradmiral Walter Hennecke and the harbor commander Fregattenkapitän Hermann Witt on June 26.

Konteradmiral Walter Hennecke, Seekommandant Normandie (center) discusses plans to demolish the port facilities of Cherbourg with the Kriegsmarine harbor commander, Fregattenkapitän Hermann Witt (left). The officer to the right is Korvettenkäpitan Weise, the commander of the MAA 260 coastal artillery battalion in the harbor area. The Gare Maritime with its 67m clock tower is visible in the background. (NARA)

## NAVAL GUN DUELS OFF CHERBOURG

The VII Corps began discussing the possibility of supporting the assault on Cherbourg with naval gunfire. This program was delayed by the massive Channel storm on the night of June 19–20 that sent many ships back to calmer waters in Britain. As a result, the bombardment was rescheduled for June 25. Collins' main intention was to eliminate the remaining

## GUN DUEL OFF CHERBOURG, JUNE 25, 1944 (PP. 68–69)

Rear Admiral Morton Deyo's Task Force 129 appeared off Cherbourg on the morning of June 25 to engage in a bombardment of German coastal gun batteries on either side of Cherbourg. Group 2 under Rear Adm. C. F. Bryant included the battleships USS *Texas* (**1**) and USS *Arkansas* (**2**) and five destroyers. Task Group 129.2 arrived in Fire Support Area 3 around 1114hrs with minesweepers in the lead. As a result, the column of ships was traveling at a dangerously slow speed.

The task group was brought under fire by MKB Hamburg (3./ MAA 26) located near Fermanville. This battery consisted of four Škoda 240mm SKL/40 guns. Only a portion of the guns were in complete concrete casemates. USS *Arkansas* begins firing on targets in the area based on the direction of Shore Fire Control Parties at 1208hrs followed by the destroyer USS *Barton* and the battleship USS *Texas* (BB-35). The German battery waits until 1229hrs when the Allied force is about 18,000m from shore. Its first targets are the minesweepers that are in the lead. During its second salvo, one of the rounds ricochets and penetrates the engine room of the *Barton*; another round strikes the anchor of the destroyer *Laffey*. Both rounds are duds and do minor damage. At 1234hrs, a 155mm howitzer of 7./Artillerie-Regiment 709 located near Les Sens strikes the port side of *Texas* near the waterline and explodes but does not penetrate. Around 1251hrs, a round from MKB Hamburg strikes near the combat information center of the destroyer O'Brien, killing 13, wounding 19, and putting the ship's radar out of action; it disengages under a smokescreen. The duel continues into the afternoon, with the battleships also engaging nearby army batteries. MKB Hamburg scores a hit on the battleship *Texas* around 1316hrs, damaging the fire control tower and bridge. Captain Charles Baker, commanding the USS *Texas*, is outside the bridge and is knocked to the deck by the impact, but not injured. Revenge is fast in coming when *Texas* manages a direct hit on the forward gun shield of Turm 1, putting it out of action. Another salvo from MKB Hamburg puts a round into the port side just below the forward wardroom, but also fails to explode. Bombardment Group 2 retires to Portland after 1500hrs. It has fired 206 14in., 58 12in., and 552 5in. rounds against the four gun casemates, managing to put only one gun out of action. The battery would be captured on June 27 by the 4th Infantry Division; in the meantime, the battery commander, Oberleutnant (MA) Rudi Gelbhaar, had been awarded the Knight's Cross. The gun duels of June 25 re-emphasized the Nelsonian adage that "A ship's a fool to fight a fort."

coastal batteries, not to engage targets in the city itself. Task Force 129 was organized under Rear Admiral Morton Deyo consisting of two groups. Bombardment Group 1 under Rear Adm. Deyo included the battleship USS *Nevada*, and the cruisers USS *Tuscaloosa*, HMS *Glasgow* and HMS *Enterprise*. Group 2 under Rear Adm. C. F. Bryant included the battleships USS *Texas* and USS *Arkansas* and five destroyers. The force was preceded by US Mine Squadron 7 and the Royal Navy 9 Minesweeping Flotilla. Air cover was provided by the IX Army Air Force.

By the time the task force arrived off Cherbourg, US troops were well into the city. Collins restricted the targets to coastal batteries away from Cherbourg to avoid fratricide. In the late morning, a Royal Navy minesweeper was engaged by MKB York, armed with four 170mm SKL/40 naval guns in full casemates, located on the coast at Querqueville. The Royal Navy cruisers HMS *Glasgow* and HMS *Enterprise* headed closer to shore and began bombarding the site with observation provided by an accompanying Spitfire. Two of the guns were quickly knocked out, but in the process the *Glasgow* was struck once in the hangar and once in aft superstructure. *Glasgow* withdrew to check damage and was called away to other sites. By mid-afternoon when HMS *Enterprise* ceased firing, both cruisers had expended 318 rounds of 6in. ammunition and all four guns were silent. However, around 1330hrs,

A scene of devastation looking out of the Gare Maritime towards the inner Cherbourg harbor with the remains of the famous clock tower in the foreground. (NARA)

the battery began firing at one of the accompanying destroyers. This led to the engagement of the cruiser USS *Tuscaloosa*, several destroyers, and eventually the battleship *Nevada*. After several explosions were spotted, the gunfire from shore seemed to cease. The flotilla departed only to receive a few more rounds from the obstreperous battery. In spite of its tenacity, MKB York was also remarkable for its poor aim.

When completed in 1933, the Gare Maritime Transatlantique was the second-largest structure in France after the Versailles palace. Aside from the damage to the railroad station itself, the Kriegsmarine demolitions also collapsed the piers into the Darse Transatlantique basin to the left to prevent the use of the pier, and sank the cargo ship *Le Normand* on the other side to block access to the commercial port behind. (NARA)

In the early afternoon, one of the destroyers was engaged by the 105mm guns of MKB Landemer to the east of Gruchy. It was engaged by HMS *Glasgow*, which fired 54 rounds starting at 1311hrs, which temporarily silenced the battery. When the battery resumed firing at 1330hrs, *Glasgow* fired 57 more rounds, followed by some 5in. destroyer fire. The battery was still firing when the warships retired.

In the late morning and early afternoon, the other elements of Bombardment Group 1 were engaging targets based on spotting by Shore Fire Control Parties. *Nevada*, *Tuscaloosa* and *Quincy* attacked targets in the western suburbs of Cherbourg shortly after noon. The destroyer USS *Emmons* moved near Cherbourg harbor and engaged in a duel with the 4.7in. guns on Fort de l'Est on the Cherbourg breakwater. It also came under

A dramatic moment as a round from MKB Hamburg lands beyond the battleship USS *Arkansas* in the wake of the USS *Texas*. The *Texas* was struck several times by the battery, but managed to knock out one of the guns during the duels on June 25. (NARA)

heavier fire, probably from Fort du Roule or one of the other harbor batteries before it withdrew. The battleship *Nevada* exchanged fire with the four guns of MKB Bastion II, located on the fortified walls of the naval arsenal on the western side of Cherbourg, before retiring.

Operating farther to the east, Bombardment Group 2 had one of the most spirited engagements of the day against MKB Hamburg. The fortified battery, armed with four 240mm guns, began firing at the minesweepers leading the group shortly after noon. The destroyer USS *Barton* was struck in the engine room; it was a dud as was another hit against the destroyer USS *Laffey*. Around 1251hrs, the combat information center of the destroyer *O'Brien* was hit, killing 13, wounding 19, and putting the ship's radar out of action. The battleships *Texas* and *Arkansas* began shelling MKB Hamburg, but the resulting dust and debris made accurate spotting very difficult. The German battery scored a hit on the battleship *Texas* around 1316hrs, damaging the fire control tower and bridge. Revenge was fast in coming when *Texas* managed a direct hit on the forward gun shield of Turm 1, putting it out of action. Bombardment Group 2 retired back to Portland after 1500hrs. They had fired 206 14in., 58 12in., and 552 5in. rounds against the four gun casemates, managing to put only one gun out of action. The battery was captured on June 27 by the 4th Infantry Division; in the meantime, the battery commander, Oberleutnant (MA) Rudi Gelbhaar, had been awarded the Knight's Cross. The gun duels of June 25 re-emphasized the Nelsonian adage that "A ship's a fool to fight a fort."

This overhead view shows MKB Hamburg in early July 1944 after its capture. The gun in the foreground is Turm Nr. 1, which used a modified casemate to permit greater traverse. It was hit during the duel with USS *Texas*. A second gun bunker can be seen in the upper right of the photo. (NARA)

# THE FALL OF FESTUNG CHERBOURG

The final assault into the city by the 9th and 79th divisions began on June 26. In anticipation of a siege, the Germans evacuated the city of most of its population. The pre-war level population of 38,000 had fallen to about 25,000 by 1944, and was reduced to only about 5,000 civilians by the evacuation.

Although the 314th Infantry was in control of the upper portions of Fort du Roule, the gun casemates on the north face of the cliffs were still under control of the 8./HKAR 1261, led by Oberleutnant zur See Rose. The extensive underground galleries at the base of the hill also remained in German hands, but were less of a threat since the garrison was largely isolated behind the armored doors covering the cave entrances. The Americans tried to lower explosive charges down through ventilation shafts and over the sides of the cliffs. A demolition team from Co. E/314th Infantry snaked its way along the cliff-face on the western side of the fort and blasted one of the tunnel openings with pole charges and bazookas. Troops below the fort began firing into the embrasures with 57mm anti-tank guns. Through the day, the German artillery crews continued to fire their guns against American troops in the streets of Cherbourg below. Resistance at Fort du Roule finally collapsed in the early evening and about 500 prisoners were taken.

A house-to-house clearing operation during the fighting for Cherbourg on June 26. (NARA)

The 39th Infantry, 9th Division pushed down the Octeville road into Cherbourg during the morning. A captured German soldier reported that the Cherbourg command bunker was located in a series of French Navy tunnels that had been carved into one of the rocky hills in St Sauveur. Companies E and F fought their way to the cave entrances of Stützpunkt 259 through the early afternoon. A prisoner was sent to one of the three armored doors covering the cave entrances with a surrender message. The surrender was refused, so a pair of M10 3in. GMC tank destroyers was driven up and began to fire directly at the three doors at point-blank range. Conditions in the tunnels had already become intolerable through overcrowding and fumes, and Schlieben agreed to surrender. A white flag was raised outside one of the doors, and eventually some 800 troops emerged including both Schlieben and Hennecke.

General Schlieben surrendered to Gen. Eddy, 9th Division commander, who insisted that he surrender the entire Cherbourg garrison. Schlieben refused and indicated that he could not do so, even if he wished, as there were no communications with the scattered and isolated garrisons. Schlieben was taken to Gen. Collins who again insisted on the surrender of the entire garrison; Schlieben again refused. The group retired to Collins' headquarters, located at the Château de Servigny in Yvetot-Bocage, west of Valognes, for a formal surrender. The last major garrison to capitulate that day was at the city hall where about 400 troops surrendered to the 2/39th Infantry.

Although most of the city was in American hands by the evening, there were still numerous pockets of resistance and scattered fighting. The most significant area still under German control on the morning of June 27 was the Arsenal de Cherbourg, the fortified naval base on the western side of the city. The extensive complex was separated from the city by a 19th-century moat and fortified walls. On the morning of June 27, the 1/39th Infantry

The surrender of the German underground headquarters at one of the tunnel entrances at Strongpoint 259 in St Sauveur on June 26. Konteradmiral Hennecke can be seen in the center. Festung Cherbourg commander, Gen.Lt. von Schlieben, wearing a steel helmet, is to the left and largely hidden behind the officer from Co. E, 39th Infantry. (NARA)

# The attack on Cherbourg: June 22–26, 1944

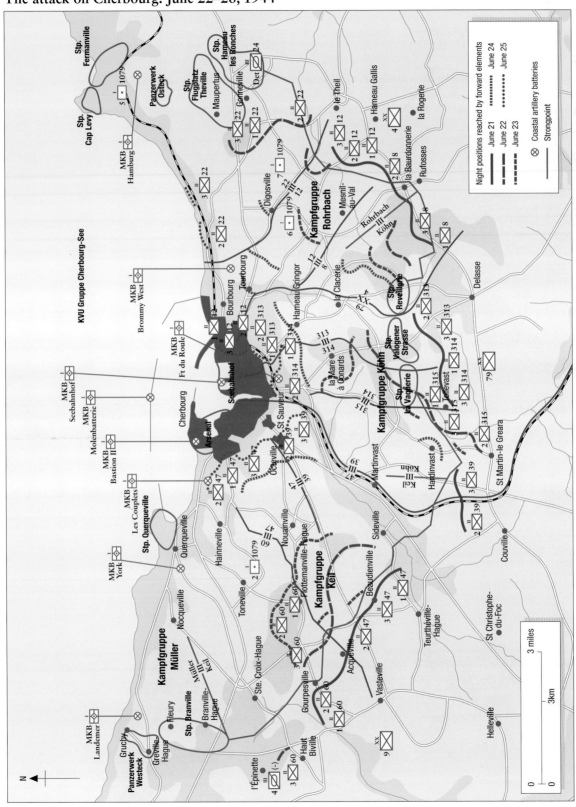

The surrender discussions on June 26 took place at Collins' headquarters in the Château de Servigny in Yvetot-Bocage near Valognes. Seen here in the foreground left to right are Konteradmiral Hennecke, the American translator (back to the camera), Gen. Schlieben, and Gen. Collins. (NARA)

began sniping at targets of opportunity and an M4 medium tank destroyed two 20mm Flak guns on the parapets. A loudspeaker team was brought up to the walls around 0830hrs, but a large concentration of personnel under the command of Gen.Maj. Robert Sattler had already decided to surrender after learning that Schlieben had capitulated the day before. White flags appeared over the walls, and Gen.Maj. Sattler led the surrender party out of the base at around 1000hrs, followed by about 400 troops.

M4 medium tanks of the 746th Tank Battalion, supporting the 39th Infantry, advance westward along Rue du Val de Saire on the morning of June 27. The tanks were heading for the arsenal, the site of the last remaining German garrison. (NARA)

**RIGHT**
A column of German prisoners is escorted out of Cherbourg along Avenue de Paris down the hill from Fort du Roule on June 28, 1944. The officer in the center of the picture is Capt. William Hooper of Co. F, 314th Infantry, 79th Division who was killed two weeks later in the fighting for Le Haye du Puits. (NARA)

**BELOW**
Following the German surrender, GIs of the 79th Division take a breather on June 28 around an abandoned war-booty Soviet 76.2mm Model 1902/30 divisional gun and its caisson in front of the Café du Rond-Point on Avenue Carnot. A battery of these old Tsarist Putilov guns, in the modernized 1930 version, was used by Witt's harbor command for local defense. In this case, it was positioned to cover a traffic circle to the east of the Bassin de Commerce harbor. (NARA)

The arsenal was enveloped in smoke, and its communication network was in tatters. Groups of German naval personnel remained isolated in buildings around the sprawling facility. Later in the day, a US Navy reconnaissance team led by Commander Quentin Walsh (USCG) began carefully working its way through the arsenal as the first step in an effort to rehabilitate the port. Armed with Thompson submachine guns and grenades, they prowled through the arsenal, uncovering scattered detachments of isolated Germans who surrendered, eventually totaling a further 500 men. The German officer holding Fort du Homet refused to surrender until Walsh threatened to attack with 800 troops. The bluff proved sufficient and the Germans in the fort emerged along with about 50 American paratroopers who had been captured on D-Day after their aircraft had dropped them on the Cotentin Peninsula. The isolated German garrisons surrendering on June 27 brought the total number of prisoners from the Cherbourg garrison to about 10,000.

The surrender of the arsenal marked the end of heavy fighting in Cherbourg, but there were still small clumps of resistance around the city. The evening before, Fregattenkapitän Witt, the harbor commander, had gathered many of the remaining Kriegsmarine officers in the arsenal for a meeting to discuss future actions. The diehards led by Witt decided to take over the forts on the Digue du Large breakwater in the harbor. Witt's groups hoped that they could further delay Allied control of Cherbourg harbor since the forts controlled several of the minefields and were well armed. Around 0330hrs in the pre-dawn hours of June 27, Witt and his group sailed from Fort du Homet over to the forts on a yacht and some whaleboats. Witt installed Leutnant zur See Reinelt to command the garrison in Fort Central while he took command of Fort de l'Ouest. The forts were armed with 4.7in. British anti-aircraft guns left behind in 1940 during the evacuation of the British Expeditionary Force. They also had 20mm and 37mm Flak cannons,

This is the naval arsenal on the western side of Cherbourg harbor. This view is looking southward over the 19th-century fortified seawalls. This particular section of the arsenal wall was guarded by the 4./MAA 260, MKB Bastion II. A careful examination of the photo will reveal the four M170 gun casemates on the top of the wall, each armed with 105mm SKC/32.U U-boat deck guns. The battery's M162a fire control bunker can be seen at the far right. This battery took part in the naval duel on June 25. The body of water seen in this view is the Bassin Napoleon III, one of three enclosed basins within the arsenal; the other two are to the east and not visible in this photo. (NARA)

and a few 50mm pedestal guns. Besides Witt's group in the two forts, some of the isolated coastal artillery batteries also had not surrendered.

On June 27, the US Navy commander, Adm. A. G. Kirk, dispatched the destroyer USS *Shubrick* and four PT boats to probe the gun batteries, while two more PT boats approached the Digue du Large. The two PT boats under Lt. Cmdr. J. D. Bulkeley came under scattered fire from the forts on the outer breakwater and began zigzagging towards the forts while firing their machine guns. This had no effect against the massive forts and within minutes one of the 4.7in. guns scored a near miss on PT-521 which left it dead in the water for a few worrisome minutes while the crew tried to get the engine restarted. They reported back that the forts were still in German hands.

On June 28, Fort Central was bombed by nine P-47 Thunderbolts. Some of the neighboring defenses, including the Digue de Querqueville and Fort de Chavanac, surrendered that day. Since Witt's force was delaying the start of minesweeping in the harbor, on June 29 Collins ordered the VII Corps artillery to dispatch five field artillery batteries to the harbor to batter the forts into submission. Witt and several other officers were wounded during the bombardment by flying slabs of granite. By late afternoon, the troops in the forts had had enough and sent out a delegation to discuss terms; they surrendered by 1900hrs.

GIs search the German troops who surrendered at Fort de l'Ouest late on June 29. This 19th-century fort had been built on the outer breakwater and modernized by the Kriegsmarine with modern guns. It was occupied by the harbor commandant, Fregattenkapitän Witt, and his band of diehards after the fall of the naval arsenal. (NARA)

# CLEARING THE EASTERN STRONGPOINTS

The coast to the east of Cherbourg was still in German hands during the battle for Cherbourg. The centerpiece of this section of the Landfront was Panzerwerk Osteck, with two other strongpoints, StP Fermanville and StP Hameau-les-Ronches to either side. This sector was commanded by Major Friedrich Küppers, previously the artillery commander on the Montebourg front. During the initial attempts by the 4th Infantry Division to penetrate the Landfront in this sector, the 22nd Infantry had been frustrated by the heavy concentration of defenses at StP Hameau-les-Ronches and the neighboring Flugplatz-Théville airbase. As a result, the regiment was assigned to contain the German forces during the battle of Cherbourg.

With the final attack into Cherbourg beginning on June 26, the 22nd Infantry was ordered to clear out the airbase and then push to the coast in the direction of Cap Lévy to the north and St Pierre-Église to the east. The 3/22nd Infantry captured the town of Maupertus and reached the northern side of the airbase, the 2/22nd Infantry reached the western edge of the airbase, and the 1/22nd Infantry captured Gonneville and reached the southern side. However, heavy fire from the numerous Flak batteries prevented the capture of Flugplatz-Théville on the first day of the attack. Word of Schlieben's surrender in Cherbourg late on June 26 was broadcast by radio and propaganda leaflets, demoralizing the German defenders in this sector. Surrender negotiations began on the morning of June 27, and most of the strongpoints surrendered by 1330hrs, with about 990 prisoners being taken. The 22nd Infantry continued to advance to the coast, and the 44th Field Artillery Battalion bombarded several remaining coastal batteries into submission. Clean-up operations on the many defense nests continued through the day, and Major Küppers surrendered shortly before midnight. Although mop-up operations continued for a few days, by June 27 all organized resistance east of Cherbourg had ended.

# CLEARING THE JOBOURG PENINSULA

Oberst Keil arrived at the Panzerwerk Westeck fortified zone on June 25 to survey the defenses. This strongpoint was manned by a fortress cadre company, while the defenses farther south were held by Oberstleutnant Müller and his battle group from GR 922. Their main defenses were located in Stützpunkt Branville, which consisted of five defense nests. This section of the Cherbourg Landfront was oriented to defend westward, but the anticipated American attack would come from Cherbourg to its east against the back of the defenses. So, for example, the large anti-tank ditch across the base of the peninsula was actually behind the defense line.

Müller had reorganized his battle group from three to two battalions following the heavy loss of troops in previous fighting. Untergruppe Müller was assigned to defend the western portion of the line from the Cherbourg–Beaumont–Hague road to the west coast. Later in the day, II./GR 919 arrived, and Keil put the battalion commander in charge of the Westeck strongpoint as Untergruppe Hadenfeldt, but extended the command so that it also incorporated the StP Branville to the south. By this stage, the battalion was down to only about 60 men. It was reinforced with remnants of Panzerjäger-

Abt. 709. The III./GR 919 arrived later, but was down to only about 80 men. It was positioned between Untergruppe Hadenfeldt and Untergruppe Müller.

The reserve for KG Keil was II./GR 920, totaling only about 80 men under the command of an NCO. A mobile reserve was formed from the five remaining French light tanks of Pz.-Abt. 100. It was apparent to Keil that his weak positions would be hit with overwhelming force, so he began creating a second and third defensive lines farther to the northwest. This included the scraps of surviving units such as the veterinary company of the 709. Infanterie-Division, the remnants of a *Fallschirmjäger* training company, a Georgian company and the survivors of Sturm-Abt. AOK 7. Keil also attempted to reinforce the various units by combining troops from assorted Luftwaffe and Kriegsmarine communication and support troops located at various sites on the coast; most companies were brought back to a strength of 80–100 men prior to the resumption of the fighting. There were still several active coastal artillery batteries in the sector, several railroad guns, and a Flak battalion. Although there was a shortage of combat troops, there was an ample supply of ammunition and weapons except for anti-tank weapons. In total, there were about 6,000 German troops on the Jobourg Peninsula.

Keil was able to communicate with higher headquarters via Luftwaffe and Kriegsmarine networks back to the Channel Islands. When asked for

The attacks on Kampfgruppe Keil on the Cap de la Hague at the end of June 1944 included bombing missions by the Ninth Air Force. This is an attack by B-26 Marauders of the 323rd Bomb Group against StP 356 at Auderville-Laye at the tip of the peninsula on June 28, 1944. This strongpoint contained the four railroad guns of the 3./ HKAR 1262 coastal battery. (NARA)

further instructions, he was simply ordered to "Hold out until the last." Well aware of the poor morale of his improvised command, he suggested that the only way to ensure a vigorous defense was to offer the men some hope, either by staging a risky breakthrough attempt towards the south, or withdrawing the garrison to the tip of the peninsula and evacuating the men by sea to the Channel Islands. Both suggestions were rebuffed by the AOK 7 headquarters. The only solace was nightly drops of supplies by transport aircraft of the Luftwaffe. Keil desperately needed trained infantry officers since many companies were being led by Kriegsmarine or Luftwaffe officers with no battlefield experience or training. An attempt was made to bring in a group from the Channel Islands via a speedboat on the night of June 27–28, but the venture was doomed in the face of the Royal Navy blockade.

Following the fall of Cherbourg, Collins began to reorganize the VII Corps forces on the Cotentin Peninsula. The 79th Division was sent south to VIII Corps to take part in the battles in that sector, while the bloodied 4th Division was given a respite to patrol Cherbourg and to clear out remaining holdouts and stragglers. This left 9th Division to deal with the Jobourg Peninsula, better known in American accounts as Cap de la Hague. The division spent most of June 27–28 regrouping for a planned attack on June 29. The 47th Infantry, on the division's right flank near the coast, was instructed to straighten out its lines in preparation for the attack, and in so

The June 28 air raids on Auderville-Laye disabled the remaining 203mm K(E) railroad guns of 3./HKAR 1262 but most of the damage was caused when the garrison spiked the ammunition stores. This is gun 919177, with another of the battery's four guns visible in the background to the left. (NARA)

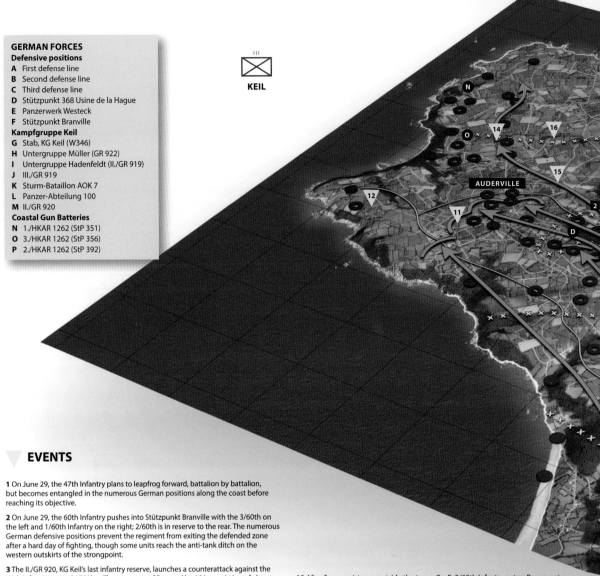

**GERMAN FORCES**

**Defensive positions**
A First defense line
B Second defense line
C Third defense line
D Stützpunkt 368 Usine de la Hague
E Panzerwerk Westeck
F Stützpunkt Branville

**Kampfgruppe Keil**
G Stab, KG Keil (W346)
H Untergruppe Müller (GR 922)
I Untergruppe Hadenfeldt (II./GR 919)
J III./GR 919
K Sturm-Bataillon AOK 7
L Panzer-Abteilung 100
M II./GR 920

**Coastal Gun Batteries**
N 1./HKAR 1262 (StP 351)
O 3./HKAR 1262 (StP 356)
P 2./HKAR 1262 (StP 392)

KEIL

AUDERVILLE

## ▼ EVENTS

**1** On June 29, the 47th Infantry plans to leapfrog forward, battalion by battalion, but becomes entangled in the numerous German positions along the coast before reaching its objective.

**2** On June 29, the 60th Infantry pushes into Stützpunkt Branville with the 3/60th on the left and 1/60th Infantry on the right; 2/60th is in reserve to the rear. The numerous German defensive positions prevent the regiment from exiting the defended zone after a hard day of fighting, though some units reach the anti-tank ditch on the western outskirts of the strongpoint.

**3** The II./GR 920, KG Keil's last infantry reserve, launches a counterattack against the 60th Infantry around 1700hrs. The remnants of Panzer-Abt. 101, consisting of about five war-booty French light tanks, supports the counterattack. The counterattack is crushed by a 20-minute "Zombie" fire mission, a concentration by all divisional field artillery.

**4** The 4th Cavalry Squadron, acting as the left flank guard, reaches as far as the stream known as the Ruisseau de la Grande Vallée.

**5** With support of M10 tank destroyers, the 2/47th Infantry begins to attack the bunkers systematically in the southern side of Panzerwerk Westeck, known as the "Gréville Fort" in US accounts. The town of Gréville is secured by 1100hrs.

**6** The 3/47th Infantry encounters substantial resistance when attacking the central portions of Panzerwerk Westeck and does not penetrate through the defenses until 1800hrs.

**7** Some bunkers at Panzerwerk Westeck have been bypassed, and the local commander, Major Hadenfeldt, remains in his command bunker until 1100hrs on July 1.

**8** The 47th Infantry pushes up to the German second line of resistance and overwhelms the battered remnants of Hptm. Kaldanke's Sturm-Bataillon AOK 7. The regiment continues towards its objectives near Digulleville. The attack leads to the collapse of the main line of German defense in this sector and 3/47th Infantry alone takes more than 500 prisoners.

**9** With the crust of the German defenses broken, 60th Infantry pushes through the remains of Stützpunkt Branville and heads for Beaumont-Hague. Oberstleutnant Müller is trapped in his command bunker southwest of the town and surrenders at 1600hrs.

**10** After fierce resistance outside the town, Co. E, 2/60th Infantry enters Beaumont-Hague and the town is cleared by Company F. A total of 58 prisoners are taken.

**11** Following the collapse of German defenses around Beaumont-Hague, the 60th Infantry nearly reaches the western coast by nightfall. The regiment captures about a 1,000 prisoners that day.

**12** The last remaining defense beyond the German second line of resistance is the veterinary company of the 709. Infanterie-Division, weakly armed with light weapons.

**13** Oberst Keil's command bunker in the Kriegsmarine defense nest W346 near Digulleville comes under fire around 2000hrs. His artillery commander, thinking that Keil has been killed by an artillery burst near the bunker entrance, presumes him dead and puts up a white flag. Keil in fact has survived and in the confusion escapes to the northwest with his driver. He is captured by an American patrol around midnight.

**14** The 9th Reconnaissance Troop heads north to Auderville, reaching the outskirts of the town in the pre-dawn hours of July 1. Reporting the route clear of serious resistance, Gen. Eddy orders a motorized infantry advance by 3/39th Infantry which is in a staging area near Beaumont-Hague.

**15** At 0400hrs on July 1, the 3/39th Infantry sets out for Auderville on trucks and makes a fast road advance. By 0500hrs, the battalion reports that it achieved complete surprise and that "everything here had given up." The battalion captures about a thousand prisoners that day.

**16** German resistance collapses on July 1 and the other elements of the 9th Division spend the day on mop-up operations. The 47th Infantry reports, "the Germans are just sitting around waiting to be taken."

# CLEARING CAP DE LA HAGUE, JUNE 29 TO JULY 1, 1944

**Note:** Gridlines are shown at intervals of 1km

Defence nests

Luftwaffe Flak/radar sites

DIGULLEVILLE

BEAUMONT-HAGUE

GRÉVILLE

BRANVILLE

N

9 ⊠ EDDY

doing overran MKB Landemer. Preparatory air strikes by P-47 Thunderbolts and B-26 Marauders knocked out the remaining railroad guns stationed on the peninsula.

The 9th Division attack began on the morning of June 29, with the 47th Infantry on the right flank facing StP Westeck, the 60th Infantry in the center facing StP Branville, and the 4th Cavalry Squadron acting as a screening force on the extreme left flank towards the west. The 47th Infantry pushed to the eastern side of StP Westeck, but was unable to overcome the strong defenses. In contrast, the 60th Infantry overran StP Branville against "moderate resistance," reaching the southern edge of the anti-tank ditch on the outside of the Landfront. A total of 426 prisoners were captured that day.

The fighting resumed on the morning of June 30, with the 60th Infantry overrunning Untergruppe Müller near Beaumont-Hague and leaving Oberstlt. Müller surrounded in his bunker. By the end of the day, the regiment had pushed through the secondary defense lines and had captured about 1,000 prisoners during the day's fighting. To the north, the 47th Infantry overcame StP Westeck against stiff resistance and pushed up to their objectives near the eastern coast of the peninsula short of Digulleville. There were still holdouts in the various bunkers in Panzerwerk Westeck, and Maj. Hadenfeldt was not captured until 1100hrs the following day. Oberst Keil was captured by an American patrol around midnight. The fighting on June 30 had completely overwhelmed all major German defenses and had netted 2,077 prisoners.

With the main defense lines overcome, on July 1, the 3/39th Infantry was put on trucks and sent on a fast road advance to secure Auderville on the northwestern tip of the peninsula. German resistance collapsed and the other elements of the 9th Division spent the day on mop-up operations. In total, some 2,984 prisoners were captured that day, and organized resistance ceased. Late on July 1, Gen. Eddy reported to Collins' VII Corps headquarters that all organized resistance on the Cotentin Peninsula had ended.

## OPENING THE PORT OF CHERBOURG

When captured, Cherbourg was useless as a port until the demolition work done by the Kriegsmarine was repaired. The original *Overlord* plans anticipated that port operations would begin three to four days after capture at a reduced level, gradually rising to 8,500 tons daily by D+90. These plans underestimated the difficulties in opening the port. Both the US Navy and US Army had prepared special detachments that entered the port area during the final stages of the battle of Cherbourg. Commodore William A. Sullivan led the Navy's salvage operation, designated as Task Group 122.2. This team had previously salvaged North African ports as well as Palermo on Sicily and Naples on the Italian mainland. The port operation was led by Col. Cleland Sibley, and managed by the 4th Port Headquarters; the engineering effort to rebuild the port was undertaken by Col. Theodore Wyman of the Cherbourg Provisional Command.

The initial US Army assessment was that the "demolition of the port of Cherbourg is a masterful job, beyond a doubt the most complete, intensive, and best-planned demolition in history." US Navy officers later described the German demolition effort as "exemplary" but that it was "more spectacular than effective." They concluded that the German demolition crews did not understand harbor operations and so demolished some key installations while missing other facilities more important to harbor functions. The railroad marshalling yards were not heavily damaged except for one of the tunnels leading into the city. The most dangerous element of the German operation was the mine-laying which was described as "unprecedentedly intricate and thorough."

The mines consisted of control mines across the entrances to the Grande Rade and Petite Rade, linked to command stations in the harbor forts. The harbor itself was strewn with no fewer than 268 mines including 74 control mines, 107 moored contact mines, 14 magnetic influence mines, three acoustic mines, and seven sweep-wire cutters, plus an unknown number of KMA (*Küstenmine-A*: coastal mine-A). Some of these mines had delayed-action fuses so that they would detonate only after a number of vessels had passed overhead. As a result, a joint force of Royal Navy and US Navy minesweepers conducted magnetic and acoustic sweeps eight times daily for 85 days to ensure that all of these mines had been neutralized. The first cleared channel to the Grande Rade was opened on July 14. Owing to the narrowness of the harbor, ten minesweeping vessels were lost and three damaged during the harbor clearing. The most dangerous mine in these operations was the simple KMA mine, nicknamed the "Katie" by Allied intelligence. A later assessment concluded that the mine-clearing operation was "the most complicated yet encountered in any harbor clearance work." The delay in opening the port was largely attributed to the effectiveness of the German mine-laying operation rather than the demolition and sunken ships.

The first Allied vessel to enter Cherbourg's Grande Rade outer harbor on July 2, 1944, was the Royal Navy Fairmile B ML138, which was being used as a minesweeper. It is seen here from the 50mm pedestal gun station in Fort de L'Ouest. Fort de Chavagnac and the Digue de Querqueville breakwater can be seen above and to the right of the launch. (NARA)

The reconstruction program began on June 28 with four initial objectives: opening the Nouvelle Plage, the beach between the arsenal and the commercial port, for DUKW amphibious trucks; the Bassin-à-Flot wet dock in the commercial port for barges; the reclamation project of filled land near the Petite Rade for discharge of railroad rolling-stock from LSTs using rolling ramps; and the Digue du Homet breakwater to allow offloading of Liberty ships and sea-trains.

Initial freight operations at Cherbourg began on July 16, 1944, by using amphibious techniques at the Grande Rade. Liberty ships used their swinging winches to offload their cargo into DUKW amphibious trucks for the subsequent trip to the beach. By early August, the harbor operations had reached the planned goal of 8,500 tons daily. As early as July 11, plans had begun to expand the objective to 20,000 tons daily by the end of September 1944. The harbor was officially declared cleared on September 29, 1944. Cherbourg also served as the continental terminal for PLUTO (Pipe Line Under The Ocean), which carried fuel from the Isle of Wight starting on August 12, 1944.

One of the first tasks after the capture of Cherbourg was clearing the numerous naval mines planted in the harbor. This joint Royal Navy/US Navy mine disposal unit is seen moving a mine into a truck for disposal after it had been lifted out of a sunken vessel near one of the docks. (NARA)

While *Overlord* planning had anticipated that Cherbourg would bear the burden of Allied logistics for only a short time, it was the mainstay of the continental port system during the period of the greatest logistic stress in the late summer and autumn of 1944. By the autumn, Cherbourg became the second most important Allied logistical port on the Continent after Marseilles. Antwerp finally opened at the end of November 1944 and the role of Cherbourg diminished. By the end of the war, Cherbourg had handled some 2.8 million tons of cargo, making it the second most important source of supplies for the US Army in the European Theater of Operations.

Until the piers and docks in Cherbourg harbor could be cleared, Liberty ships and other cargo vessels had their shipments transferred into DUKW amphibious trucks for delivery to shore. (NARA)

# AFTERMATH

Once Cherbourg harbor was cleared of mines, larger vessels such as LSTs (landing ship tanks) could unload cargo on beaches within the harbor area. To expedite shipment, the LSTs delivered loaded railroad freight cars to a rail-line created at the water's edge. (NARA)

The capture of the port of Cherbourg was the first major Allied victory following the D-Day landings in Normandy. The fall of Cherbourg shocked Hitler and the senior German leadership in Berlin who believed that such a heavily fortified city could hold out for months. They seriously overestimated the paper strength of their own forces and seriously underestimated the combat efficiency of the US Army. With the capture of the Cotentin Peninsula, hope evaporated that the Allies could be dislodged from France.

The fighting was not as unbalanced as some later campaigns, with five US divisions facing four German divisions. Neither side had large armored forces, though the US Army had a slight advantage in this respect. Both sides had ample artillery, with the Germans having some advantages at various points in the campaign because of their large number of coastal artillery and flak batteries, while the US Army sometimes had an advantage because of their naval gunfire support. The German forces had advantages in fortified defenses but disadvantages in troop quality. The US had significant advantages in air power.

From a command perspective, Collins had greater tactical flexibility than his German counterparts and exercised it with considerable skill. He did not dither when confronted by the poor performance of the 90th Division and quickly substituted the 9th Division for the critical mission to cut off the Cotentin Peninsula. The German command situation was far more difficult. Micromanagement from Berlin by both Hitler and the OKW slowed critical decision-making and contributed to the decimation of Kampfgruppe Hellmich and the costly delay in the withdrawal into the Cherbourg Landfront. General Marcks had little tactical flexibility because of interference from Berlin as well as Rundstedt's, Rommel's, and Dollmann's headquarters; his death early in the campaign left a command void at a critical stage of the fighting.

Casualties on both sides were heavy. The US VII Corps suffered 12,969 casualties in its infantry divisions and corps troops. The two airborne divisions suffered a further 9,150 casualties but 4,478 of these were missing and many were accounted for later. The VII Corps captured 39,000 German prisoners from June 6 to July 1, and total German casualties were probably in excess of 55,000; precise figures are lacking. The intensity of the fighting in the bocage proved alarming. The US 4th Infantry Division suffered 5,452 casualties in less than three weeks of fighting, a hint of the horror to come in July 1944 in the "Green Hell" of the bocage country around St Lô.

**US VII Corps casualties, D-Day to July 1, 1944**

| Unit | Killed | Wounded | Missing | Captured | Total |
| --- | --- | --- | --- | --- | --- |
| 4th Div. | 844 | 3,814 | 788 | 6 | 5,452 |
| 9th Div. | 301 | 2,061 | 76 | | 2,438 |
| 79th Div. | 240 | 1,896 | 240 | | 2,376 |
| 90th Div. | 386 | 1,979 | 34 | | 2,399 |
| Corps troops | 37 | 157 | 49 | 61 | 304 |
| 82nd Abn. Div. | 457 | 1,440 | 2,571 | 12+ | 4,480 |
| 101st Abn. Div. | 546 | 2,217 | 1,907 | ? | 4,670 |
| **Total** | **2,811** | **13,564** | **5,665** | **79** | **22,119** |

# THE BATTLEFIELD TODAY

The demise of transatlantic steamship travel has diminished Cherbourg's importance in international travel. The port remains active for cross-Channel ferries running from Portsmouth and to the Channel Islands. The port still serves as a French Navy base, so some areas of the city, especially the Porte Militaire (arsenal), are closed to the public. One of the buildings on Fort du Roule has been converted into the "Musée de la Libération" and offers a superb view of the city below. A useful comparison of wartime versus contemporary Cherbourg is provided in the ever-useful *After the Battle* magazine, which devoted Number 147 (2010) to the battle for Cherbourg.

A view from one of the R671 SK gun casemates on the cliff-side of Fort du Roule overlooking the port of Cherbourg. (Alain Chazette)

The remains of the Atlantikwall fortifications are still quite visible along the coast. Some of the most impressive fortifications are the Marcouf/Crisbecq and Azeville batteries and there is a museum (La Batterie d'Azeville) open in the summer months. The Atlantikwall fortifications are better documented than the Landfront bunkers. Although many Landfront bunkers still exist, they are gradually disappearing year by year and are often on private land, and difficult to find.

The MKB Marcouf is preserved as a museum site today. This is a view of the second R638 casemate which was demolished by US engineers on August 21, 1944, after placing a large explosive charge inside ammunition magazines that collapsed the rear of the roof. In the foreground is the original kettle emplacement where the gun was first located before the construction of the bunker in 1944. (Author's photograph)

# FURTHER READING

The American side of the Cherbourg campaign is well covered in the two official histories by Rupprecht and Harrison. There is no comprehensive account from the German perspective though there is spotty coverage in the US Army's Foreign Military Studies. Schlieben's and Keil's accounts are by far the best of the bunch. German military records for the divisions fighting on the Cotentin Peninsula were mostly lost during the war, though there is a fair amount of information in the 7. Armee war diary (*Kriegstagebuch der Führungsabteilung AOK 7 6.-30 Juni 1944*). A microfilm copy is available in Record Group 242 at the US National Archives and Records Administration in College Park, MD, and Reardon's book provides an excellent summary in English. The records of the US Army VII Corps and its component divisions can be found in RG 407 at NARA; the "Combat Interviews" in this collection are noteworthy for an especially thorough account of the 4th Infantry Division during the campaign. The US Army Military History Institute (MHI) at the Army Historical Experiences Center at Carlisle Barracks, Pennsylvania, also has considerable material dealing with the Cherbourg campaign. Allied signals intelligence on the Cherbourg front is well covered in a separate appendix in the classic Hinsley study.

*Government studies*
Maddaloni, Gabrielle, *Liberation and Franco-American Relations in Post-War Cherbourg*, Command and General Staff School (2008)
Pederson, Maynard, et al., *Armor in Operation Neptune: Establishment of the Normandy Beachhead*, Armored School, Ft Knox (1949)
*Cherbourg – Gateway to France: Rehabilitation and Operation of the First Major Port*, History Section, ETOUSA (1946)
*First United States Army-Report of Operations 20 October 1943–1 August 1944*, multiple volumes, US Army (1946)
*US Army foreign military studies*
Keil, Günther, *Grenadier Regiment 919, Kampfgruppe Keil*, (C-018)
Keil, Günther, *Kampfgruppe Keil*, (B-844)
Koenig, Eugen, *91st Airborne Division Operations in Normandy (10 July–August 1944)*, (B-010)
Mauer, E., *The 243rd Infantry Division, Mar–Jun 1944*, (D-382)
Schlieben, Karl-Wilhelm von, *The German 709th Infantry Division during the Fighting in Normandy*, (B-845)


*Books*
Bernage, Georges, *La Bataille du Cotentin 9–19 juin 1944*, Heimdal (2013)
Bernage, Georges, *Première Victoire Américaine en Normandie*, Heimdal (1990)
Breuer, William, *Hitler's Fortress Cherbourg: The Conquest of a Bastion*, Stein & Day (1984)
Carell, Paul, *Invasion! They're Coming*, E. P. Dutton (1962)
Chazette, Alain, *Mur de l'Atlantique: Les batteries de côte en Normandie*, Histoire et Fortifications (2011)
*The Cross of Lorraine: A Combat History of the 79th Infantry Division, June 1942–December 1945*, US Army (1946)
Colby, John, *War from the Ground Up: The 90th Division in WWII*, Nortex (1991)
Collins, J. Lawton, *Lightning Joe*, LSU Press (1979)
Harrison, Gordon, *Cross-Channel Attack*, US Army Center for Military History (1951)
Havers, R. P. W., *Battlezone Normandy: Battle for Cherbourg*, Sutton (2004)
Hinsley, F. H., et al., *British Intelligence in the Second World War, Vol. 3, Part 2*, HMSO (1988)
Ingouf-Knocker, Paul, *Cotentin 44: La bataille de Cherbourg*, Albatros (1991)
Isby, David, *Fighting the Invasion: The German Army from D-Day to Villers Bocage*, Greenhill (2001)
Keugsgen, Helmut-Konrad von, *Les canons de Saint-Marcouf*, Heimdal (2005)
Lodieu, Didier, *La 90th US Inf. Div. Tome 1: Juin 1944*, Mémorial Montormel (2013)
Mittelman, Joseph, *Eight Stars to Victory: A History of the Veteran Ninth US Infantry Division*, US Army (1948)
Morison, Samuel, *History of US Naval Operations in World War II: The Invasion of France and Germany 1944–1945*, Little, Brown (1957)
Rawson, Andrew, *Battleground Europe: Cherbourg*, Pen & Sword (2004)
Reardon, Mark (ed.), *Defending Fortress Europe: The War Diary of the German 7th Army in Normandy, 6 June to 26 July 1944*, Aberjona (2012)
Rose, Yannick, *L'Artillerie Côtière de l'Est Cotentin: HKAR 1261*, ACREDIC (1995)
Rupprecht, Robert, *Utah Beach to Cherbourg*, US Army Center for Military History (1946)batteries on both sides of the Cotentin Peninsula, extensive defenses in the immediate Cherbourg area, and a *Landfront* defense to the south of the city. On February 4, 1944, Hitler declared Cherbourg to be a *Festung* (fortress), which would be defended to the last man.

# INDEX

References to illustrations are in **bold**.